TAKEN FROM THE NIGHT EXPANDED EDITION

A WITCH'S ENCOUNTER WITH GOD

S. A. TOWER

DWELL

"*A Witch's Encounter with God* is one of the most transparent and enlightening testimonies I've ever read. S.A. Tower communicates with amazing detail, the life events that drew her into the Craft and displays God's supernatural power and the extreme lengths He will go to redeem and restore. As a result of reading this book, you will be better equipped to effectively minister to those coming out of spiritual darkness. S.A. Tower is a living testament that we serve a God that never gives up on us, even when we throw in the towel or when others do."

–**Rev. Samuel Rodriguez**,
President – NHCLC, Conela
and the best-selling author of *Be Light*

"*A Witch's Encounter with God* engages the reader immediately and transports them to the battlefield of the soul. A young woman became entangled with a coven of white witchcraft and her ensuing journey to be delivered. This compelling narrative pulls no punches about church life, family struggles, and the darkness that often parades as light!"

- **Dr. Ron Phillips**,
Senior Pastor of Abba's House and
author of over 30 books, including *Our Invisible Allies*

"*A Witch's Encounter with God* is a powerful and "no-holds-barred" memoir of an ex-witch who experiences God's relentless love and grace, in spite of our flawed humanity. This book is an insightful view of the spiritual battle through the eyes of one who actually lived it, being transformed from eternal darkness to everlasting light."

- **Michael Leehan**, author of *Ascent From Darkness*

A Witch's Encounter With God

Expanded Edition

© 2017 by S. A. Tower

Published by Dwell Publishing LLC
dwellpublishing@gmail.com

Printed in the United States of America

Library of Congress Cataloging-in-Publication Data is on file at the Library of Congress, Washington, D.C.

ISBN: 978-0-9849523-0-4 (first edition, pbk)

Scripture quotations are from the New King James Version of the Bible. Copyright © 1979, 1980, 1982 by Thomas Nelson, Inc. publishers.

This story is based on true events, but certain names, persons, characters, places, and dates have been changed so that the persons and characters portrayed bear no resemblance to the persons actually living or dead.

Cover design by David Munoz

Parental discretion is advised

To Abba Father, in whom there is no greater love.

*In memory of my earthly father, who gave
me a loving example here on this earth.*

*And to my spiritual father, for adhering to
the heart of our Heavenly Father
in simply loving me.*

CONTENTS

FOREWORD

T his book vividly demonstrates how seducing spirits work on a person to turn from truth to the counterfeit. Spiritual discouragement followed by fascination of the dark arts is a masterful ploy of the Devil in these last days. Ephesians 4:27 warns us not to even give a toe-hold to the enemy!

There is a wonderful realization that God's Spirit and the Truth do not turn us loose in time of dark passages, but continue to confront us with eternal decisions.

Much of the battle is fought in the mind and emotions. When every thought is brought into subjection to the Living Word, as is so effectively brought out in this power-packed book, things begin to realign and come into God's working order again.

Congratulations on a well narrated story that will surely begin the journey back to the Cross for many wanderers in an age of rising witchcraft and paganism! I trust this will just be one of many more masterpieces to come.

~ Dr.Carol Hansen-Robeson,

Co-author of Strongman's His Name,
What's His Game? I and II

ACKNOWLEDGMENTS

To my children, thank you for allowing me the time to do what God has put on my heart... in you, I am reminded of His love and mercy.

To my special friend, thank you for always being there for me, for a continuous supply of Godly "stuff" and for your relentless persistence.

To all of the pastors who prayed, interceded and encouraged me through the different seasons of my life; especially my pastor who extended grace and continually reminded me of that October day when the angels in heaven rejoiced. And to my long distance pastor who welcomed me into his home and church, giving me what I needed... more of Jesus; you know who you are.

To my friends in Massachusetts, who have been beacons of light in finding my way out of the darkness. Blessed be in Jesus!

To my computer techs who have managed to save the contents of this manuscript on numerous occasions. Without you, much would be lost in cyber-space.

I'd like to express gratitude to Avodah Editorial Services and my editors whose expertise and concise copyediting fashioned *A Witch's Encounter with God* into a more eloquent book than I had imagined.

To all the prayer warriors, known and unknown, who have prayed for me over the years, this is the evidence in the power of prayer.

Above all, I'd like to express my adoration to Jesus, who is the author of my salvation and who clothed me in His robe of righteousness... This is the day!

PROLOGUE

Ring.

Ring.

The phone's repetitious sound roused my semi-conscious mind.

Ring. Ring. Ring.

I wanted to react, but my brain wasn't transmitting to my body.

The ringing grew louder.

Finally, my limbs succumbed to my will. Gaining control, I struggled to my hands and knees. The room spun, nauseating me, but determined, I pulled myself up to stand.

It took all my energy to stumble into the kitchen and pick up the receiver. Only a dial tone. Feeling light-headed, I propped myself against the wall and dialed everyone who might have been trying to reach me. Only my dad answered, but he hadn't called.

I looked at the clock. Three p.m.

Needing to shower before my son awoke from his nap, I made my way to the stairs and then clung to the handrail as I climbed what seemed like Mount Everest. Once in the bathroom, I undressed, turned on the water, and stepped into the shower. My fingers caught as I ran them through my hair, which strangely already felt wet and clumped together. I lowered one hand to find blood all over it.

I'm bleeding. Why am I bleeding?

The water cascaded through my hair until it ran clean, and I got out of the shower and stood in front of the mirror to examine my head for a wound. There wasn't one. Not even a scratch.

Feeling dizzy and with my head throbbing, I got dressed and went to the staircase. Then I noticed blood on the carpet at the foot of the stairs. That triggered a flashback of my body lying motionless on the floor and the mysterious conversation.

Several voices engaged in deliberation, though I couldn't see anyone. At first, I was a silent listener, and then one voice asked me a question. I vaguely remember it's wording, but the answer I gave remains vivid: "No. I don't want to leave my children."

Another voice advised that there would be much suffering and pain in my life if I stayed, but my answer remained the same: "I don't want to leave my son. And what about the baby I'm carrying?"

I sensed that all would be well with the children, then was told that if I remained, I would go into the enemy's territory, although I wouldn't lose my salvation.

"I need to be here for my children," I insisted. "I don't want to go."

Once again, I found myself staring at the blood on the floor. *What does it mean—that I'll go into the enemy's territory?* I wondered. *After all, there's no way I'll ever walk away from Jesus.*

CHAPTER ONE

—〰—

Six years later ...

When Cujo woke me that morning with his slobbery tongue on my cheek, I had no idea that this would be the day that convinced me that God had abandoned me.

After gathering the kids and handing them a makeshift breakfast, we piled into the car, which had just enough gas to drive Michael to work and the rest of us to the school bus yard. Only the hum of the engine and the kids munching on Pop-Tarts accompanied us. Michael drove, his eyes fixated on the white line in the center of the road.

Breaking the ice, I asked Michael if he had taken care of the shut-off notice for the electric bill.

He shrugged his shoulders, mumbling, "It's paid."

His response wasn't exactly reassuring. If I came home to find the power off and the food in our freezer thawing, it wouldn't be the first time.

Twenty minutes later, we arrived at Michael's work.

"Pick me up at 4:30," he said and got out.

An attractive young woman waited to greet him at the door, and they smiled and laughed as they disappeared down the hall-way together.

By the time the kids and I reached the bus yard, jealousy had hardened my heart. Once behind the wheel, I turned the key in the ignition, and the roar of its diesel engine echoed throughout the bus. For my young children, this was a welcome ride, one of the benefits of having Mom be the bus driver. They went along for the morning runs, sitting in the front seat. After making my drop-off at the last school, I drove my own children to King of Kings Christian School, where they attended. Then I had a few hours of anticipated time to myself until the next bus run.

I drove home on auto-pilot. Where had my life gone so off course? I had expected my children would grow up in the same loving environment that I had. My father was a caring dad and husband who spent quality time with his kids, and every day he told my mom how much he loved her. Each night after dinner, he and Mom would watch television, cuddled in each other's arms, and they always kissed good-night.

I couldn't remember the last time Michael kissed me.

I parked the bus in our driveway and made my way to the house, hoping we still had electricity. When I opened the door, Cujo greeted me, wagging his tail. The clock on the wall was still ticking, so the power was still on—so far.

I grabbed the phone and called Michael, but it was his co-worker who answered.

"Michael's busy," she snapped in her usual irritated tone. "I'll tell him you called." Then she hung up.

I knew she wouldn't relay the message. And what right did this woman have in screening my husband's calls? Had they become more than friends?

I couldn't help but question Michael's faithfulness. The last time I'd attempted a night of romance, I had the curtains drawn, candlelight filling the room, and soft romantic music playing in the background. Dressed in the lacy burgundy negligee he had bought me years before and with his favorite perfume dabbed on, I called for Michael to come to our bedroom. He entered the room, and by the glazed look in his eyes, he wasn't pleased with the atmosphere I had tried so hard to create.

Determined not to be discouraged, I took him in my arms.

He barely responded to the touch of my fingers running through his hair or the softness of my lips on his, but I attempted to stir some element of passion within him.

Then Michael pulled away and said he had work to do.

As he left the room, I silently screamed, *What's wrong with me? Why doesn't he desire me anymore?* My eyes teared up, and I made my way to the bathroom to get a tissue. When I glanced in the mirror, I saw a miserable woman with dark circles under her eyes. I had gained twenty pounds since becoming a mother and looked so unattractive. No wonder Michael wasn't interested in me.

A knock at the door and Cujo's barking startled me from my thoughts. I tried to gain my composure as I went to answer it. The postman stood there with a certified letter, and I almost wished I hadn't opened the door.

Once he was gone, I opened the envelope. The word *foreclosure* caught my eye, and I panicked. The day I'd dreaded had finally come. I had done as our church told me to do—trust Michael with the finances —and now we'd be out on the street.

Where would we find a place for three kids, a dog, and three cats? Since we'd bought the house, I'd thought our days of being vagabonds were over. Now I relived the nightmare of the day years before when I'd found out Michael had emptied our savings account. Only when I was about to report it as a forgery did he admit to withdrawing the balance of our wedding money that we were saving for a down payment. When we finally purchased our home, we had to resort to having my parents front the money. I had submitted to my husband as the church taught was godly order, but in reality I was at the mercy of his poor choices and the repercussions they had on my family.

Now Michael was sure to dump on me the responsibility to come up with the money to stop the foreclosure, as he always did. I couldn't ask my parents for help again and drain their savings. My next thought was to call Pastor John and Joan, my spiritual parents who actively spoke into my life. Pastor John was the senior pastor of New Zion Christian Fellowship, the spirit-filled church we attended, and he was counseling Michael about being the king, priest, and prophet of the household, and being in control of the finances.

But the harder Michael was pressured to step into his so-called God-given role, the more he became reclusive. I'd had numerous discussions with Joan, Pastor John's wife, and found it difficult to understand how Michael's lack of leadership in the home was somehow my fault because of my lack of faith. All the years I prayed and fasted seemed fruitless, and I was told I didn't pray hard enough because if I did, God would have answered my prayers.

Joan often quoted Psalm 37:4: "Delight yourself also in the LORD, and He shall give you the desires of your heart" (NKJV). And since my desires were not being met and God's Word was true, that meant the blame fell on me. I had yielded my life under the church's authority and submitted to my husband's leadership but lost all control in the process.

The foreclosure notice hit the floor as I hurled my wedding ring across the room. Tears streamed down my face, and in helplessness I cried out, "Where are you, God?" Sobbing, I looked toward heaven. "Please, Lord, show me a sign that you're here."

My cries echoed throughout the house only to return without a response.

I clenched my fists until my fingernails dug into my palms. "Why aren't you answering me, God? I desperately need you, like never before!" I tried to quiet my weary soul so I could hear the whisper of His voice, but that hope was also unfulfilled.

I fell to my knees and remembered Gideon in the Bible. "I beg you to show me a sign. Lord, I put this fleece before you—send a pastor to my door and I'll know you haven't left me." I listened, hoping for a knock on the door, but time passed until the expectation seemed pointless.

Collapsing onto my stomach with my forehead in my hands, I cried a puddle on the hardwood floor beneath me. In between sobs, I gasped for air. "God," I moaned, "why have you left me in such a desperate state?"

As I lay there, I decided that God must have chosen to ignore my cries for help. I mustered up enough strength to lift myself off the floor, frantically searching for that essence of survival. My hope in God dissipated, and I tried to convince myself that I could do this on my own. I'd always been strong and independent, able to stand on my own. Now I had only two choices: switch into survival mode or roll over and die. I chose the former and searched for inner strength. I knew it was buried deep inside me, beneath all that I'd surrendered to God, my husband, and the church.

I vowed to reclaim it.

A WITCH'S ENCOUNTER WITH GOD

CHAPTER TWO

—⟨⟨⟨—

The scent of lemon seemed intoxicating as I wiped the shelves with a terry dust cloth. The bookcase in the living room corner was packed with an assortment of books ranging from Steven King thrillers to the Bible. All was quiet with the kids in school and Michael at work. I did what I could to tidy up the house by squeezing in chores between bus runs.

As I dusted the books, one mysteriously fell off the shelf. I knelt and picked it up, taking in the cover bearing a red-robed figure and a cauldron, as well as the tattered, yellowing pages. Michael had bought this book, titled *The Satan Seller*, before we were married, but I'd never had any interest in reading it—until now. All I knew was that it was about someone who had been involved in the occult but then found God and became a Christian.

Maybe it was curiosity or my doubt in God's Word that enticed me, but I sat on the couch and began to read this man's life story. He claimed that once he became a high priest, he had unlimited wealth and power at his disposal.

Attaining wealth was immediately tempting, and I contemplated how we would get out of our financial black hole. Just as alluring was the thought of taking back power over my life. I could reclaim control over what I had forsaken to God and the men in my life.

The book continued with the gruesome details of a cat sacrifice and finger dismemberment as a part of the author's ritual. He claimed he had been "left for dead" by his cult friends, but it sounded to me like he had simply overdosed. Of course, his user friends weren't going to stick around at the hospital for fear of being arrested.

His claims seemed bizarre, and I questioned their fidelity. Was this just another Christian attempt to feed the fire of fear to scare people into the kingdom of God? Was this stuff really dangerous? Obviously, the promises of good things for those who love God hadn't materialized in my life, so why should I believe the so-called dangers of the occult?

I looked at my watch and jumped up. Time had passed much quicker than I thought, almost making me late for my afternoon runs. I put the book back on the shelf, gave Cujo a pat on the head, and grabbed my keys on the way out the door. Tomorrow I would go to the library in between runs and get out some real occult books so I could confirm this man's story.

The next day, instead of going home between runs, I went to the library. Once inside, I took a deep breath and apprehensively made my way down to the occult section. I browsed through books that dealt mostly with the history of witchcraft, some dating back to the 1700s, and selected a few. Once they were checked out, I scooped up the books, hid them beneath my hoodie, and hurried out the door.

—⁂—

That evening after Michael dropped us off at home, he headed to the grocery store in what had become his daily ritual. I turned on the radio and tuned it to the classic rock station, hoping to hear Fleetwood Mac, my favorite band from my high school days. After a news and weather break, I waited in anticipation of one of their songs. At last, "Dreams" hit the airwaves, and I danced and sang with reckless abandon.

As I spun around, Michael startled me. He had returned earlier than expected. "What are you listening to that stuff for?" he demanded. "I'll not have that kind of music in my house!"

"Your house? I thought this was our house," I said as I turned off the radio.

"I've already talked with Pastor John and he agrees with me. You know rock music is satanic." He went into the kitchen and dropped the groceries on the table.

"It's just music, Michael!" I called.

"You heard me! Don't let me find you listening to that again!"

My face flushed with heat as my heart beat faster. "Or what? Am I grounded? Since when do you give a damn about this house?" I grabbed my purse and stormed out the door. Who did he think he was, telling me what music I couldn't listen to, as if he suddenly cared what Pastor John thought. When was the last time he picked up his Bible or joined us at church? Besides, if he cared so much about the home, why didn't he pay the mortgage?

I walked past my children who were playing in the yard, let them know I'd be back shortly, and hopped in the car. After finding the same station, I cranked up the volume and drove off.

At a nearby park, I got out and kicked stones out of my way as I walked down the gravel path. It felt good to be out of the house, away from Michael's legalistic control. Water trickled over rocks in the nearby stream, and after finding a clearing, I took a seat in my outdoor sanctuary.

The setting sun cast golden rays through the trees to the grass around me. All was still except for the warm breeze that blew strands of hair into my face. My heart rate slowed to the rhythm of the water cascading over the rocks, and as I watched the water flow downstream, I longed to be carefree, moving without resistance.

My eyes followed the tree roots up the long trunk and high above the branches at the treetop. The clear sky reached to infinity, and I wondered where God was. Was He looking down, or had He completely forsaken me?

—w—

On Wednesday evening, I hung up the phone after talking to my mom. We had discussed my current mortgage dilemma, and she offered to help one last time on one condition—that we surrender the mortgage book and have Michael make biweekly payments to her. Mom would make sure the payments reached the mortgage company and didn't get lost in Michael's black hole. Going to Michael, I explained her proposition.

"I guess so," he finally said. "I don't know how I'm going to do it, but what other choice is there?"

"Well, it's this or the street," I shot back, annoyed that he wasn't grateful for Mom bailing us out. Returning to the phone, I called Mom back and let her know that Michael agreed. We made plans for us to pick up the three-months-past-due check.

The next night was prayer meeting. Instead of getting ready for a night of ritualistic prayer that I now found boring because of my unbelief, I opted to stay at home and work on my poetry. I had saved the poetry I wrote in high school until I became born again. That summer I attended a youth retreat, and upon returning home, I built a bonfire and burned all my belongings that supposedly didn't glorify God. Hundreds of albums, posters, and even my poetry all fell victim to the flames. It seemed like a wise decision at the time.

Now I wondered why I had bought into the notion that these things were evil. At least my searching for inner strength had brought back the desire to be creative. I picked up my pencil and wrote the first line of a new poem, which ironically was about Michael: *When I met you I was innocent, and we fell in love on the rock by the sea.* It felt good to express my feelings on paper again and see how the words just flowed out of me like they used to.

When I took a break from my writing, I went downstairs to wash some dishes. I gazed out the kitchen window and caught a glimpse of the magnificent full moon illuminating the sky in a way I had never noticed before. After drying my hands, I hurried out the door to find an open space where I could get a better view.

When I emerged from the trees around the house, there was the enormous moon in all its magic. I stood in awe beneath its brilliant glow, experiencing an overwhelming desire for the ancient wisdom I thought had disappeared hundreds of years ago. The bright light encircled me, its energy flowing through me, and I called upon the Goddess to reveal this ancient knowledge to me, not knowing if there was indeed a proper way to do so.

Back inside, my children asked why my face seemed to be glowing. Fortunately, it was their bedtime so I quickly tucked them in for the night and retreated to the comfort of my bedroom. I sensed that night was the beginning of something big. A passage was opening to an ancient way of life that, up to that point, I had only read about and dreamt of finding.

On my way home from the morning bus run the next day, I stopped at the pharmacy looking for a magazine to read while waiting for school dismissals. I found one and flipped to the back page to find an advertisement that read, *Seekers ... of Witchcraft*. Whoa! This was the answer I'd been waiting for. I bought the magazine, rushed home, and wrote a letter to the source in the magazine, then drove to the post office, opened a PO box, and sent the letter using my new address.

Before the moon had completed its cycle, I received a reply and enrolled in a school of witchcraft. Wicca, as some call it, is a pagan religion dating back to pre-Christian times. My first lesson was on the philosophy of the Craft, and I was thrilled to discover the school had their own library, especially since I'd quickly exhausted the resources in mine.

One of the first things I learned was not to take anything that was said as law. I was encouraged to research and discover my own truth— which I found very appealing and much different from my church's approach to truth. I then read *When God Was a Woman* by Merlin Stone (from the recommended reading list), which is an archaeologically documented story of the religion of the Goddess. The book explained that the priests and men from Judeo-Christian times destroyed the temples in which the Goddess was worshiped, and built their own temples, creating stories in the Bible claiming the Goddess to be evil in their deliberate attempt to gain control of women's wealth and property.

Glancing up from my reading, I looked out the bus window to Our Lady of Sorrows, the Catholic school where I was waiting. I thought of the many Goddess worshipers that had taken cover in ancient abbeys to avoid the persecution of men—men just like Michael and Pastor John, who had become two more in a long line of oppressors.

As I immersed myself in my studies, I also discovered a belief system based on living in harmony with nature and honoring all things inhabiting the earth and the spirit world. I gained a new appreciation for the earth, and joined Greenpeace's mailing list and began recycling to save the planet. Plastic holders from six-packs of soda were cut so dolphins wouldn't get their snouts caught in them once they were dumped in the ocean, and I developed a great interest in gardening, which quickly became more than just planting flowers.

Soon I had created a perfect little witch garden where I could spend my free time caring for the tiny seedlings and watching them grow. After harvesting according to the correct moon phase, such as digging roots during the waning moon, I would hang them for drying before storing them in jars for future use in portions or spells. Along with herbs, I collected crystals and stones for their magical energies. It was my research about these stones and their uses that brought the first real sign of trouble in my newfound lifestyle.

CHAPTER THREE

—◊—

I walked in the back door to find Michael waiting for me with a folded piece of paper in his hand. His steady gaze caught my attention even though I tried to keep my eyes from meeting his. He stood tall and self-assured as he approached me.

"What's this?" he asked as he held up my notes on the magical uses of stones and crystals.

I tried to shrug it off as no big deal, knowing he would view the magical use of anything as evil.

"I already talked with Pastor John about this. I think you'd best have a talk with him."

"Where are the kids?" I asked, momentarily putting him off while searching for an answer.

Michael told me they were playing, which was immediately confirmed by the laughter coming from upstairs. He gave me back my notes, saying, "He's expecting to hear from you tonight," then grabbed his coffee and retreated upstairs.

I sighed. So what if I was reading about crystals? What right did he have to go through my belongings? Why the concern now when he hadn't cared about me for years? I knew the church would not view this as a positive thing to occupy my time with. Suddenly I thought of my books on witchcraft. What if he'd found them instead of my notes on stones and crystals? I had been fortunate this time, but I'd have to be a lot more careful about what I left lying around.

Frantically, I searched for a place to hide my things away from prying eyes. I could think of only one place—my workstation, the school bus I drove. Having settled that in my mind, I picked up the phone and called Pastor John.

Our conversation was one I wasn't looking forward to. Pastor John oversaw the deliverance ministry at New Zion, and they considered all occult activity as demonic, separating themselves from any involvement whatsoever. Under their teaching, I had been forewarned about opening myself to occult influences, but at this point I believed many of their teachings to be dogmatic and closed-minded. Crystals and their magical purpose would certainly be considered evil in their eyes, but I questioned myself, *Does everything in the universe have a demon attached to it?*

Waiting for Pastor John to answer the phone, all I could think about was how I was becoming a disappointment to him. I knew well his personal commitment and dedication to God, and he expected the same from his church members. With each ring, I hoped no one would answer and I could just leave a voicemail. I paced back and forth as far as the cord would allow, all the while wrapping it nervously around my finger. How would I explain why I had instructions on the magical use of stones? And what had Michael told him?

On the tenth ring, just as I was about to hang up, the click of the receiver being picked up came through the line. "Hello, John speaking."

The conversation went pretty much the way I had figured it would. He said that I was venturing into dangerous territory and he was genuinely concerned for my spiritual well-being. Apparently, it was all right to ask questions, but he warned against delving into things that were not of God. The conversation ended with him asking me to promise I'd refrain from any further dabbling in the occult, but it was a promise I couldn't make.

—⁂—

At the break of dawn on Sunday, I was roused from my sleep

by a rumbling sound on the floor upstairs. Michael was gone, and I assumed he was down at the corner deli partaking in his weekend "shooting the bull" ritual over coffee. It sounded like a wild animal had gotten trapped in the attic and panicked in its attempt to get out. Loud thuds and the sound of items being tossed to and fro put me on edge as I worried about my children's safety.

I flung back the sheets and grabbed the hammer from under the bed, then tiptoed my way to the bedroom door. Footsteps came down the attic stairs, and I shook as I stood with the hammer raised and turned the doorknob to find ... Michael. He had a dusty backpack and sleeping bag under his arm and a faded tent on his shoulder.

"What are you doing?" I asked. "You scared me half to death."

"I went up to the attic to get the camping stuff." He then informed me that he was leaving to get my coffee and roll. As he headed downstairs with the gear and I retreated to the bedroom, I thought about how we had been the outdoors type before we were married. We hadn't talked about camping in years.

A few minutes later, I headed downstairs to find Michael loading the washer. He then wiped down his old backpack. I asked what he was doing.

"Some of my coworkers are going camping next weekend. I was thinking of joining them."

Hope welled in me. "Well, I can ask my mom to take the kids for the weekend to free us up to go. I'm sure the kids would love a weekend at Grandma and Grandpa's."

He fumbled through his backpack, pulling out a canteen, whistle, and flashlight. Finally, he said, "I'm not going, but I'll take this in so my coworkers can borrow it. This stuff is expensive to buy."

"It would be nice for us to get away without the kids," I pointed out.

Michael didn't say a word, which in turn said it all.

—⟋⟍—

Two hours later, the kids and I pulled into the nearly full parking lot of Washington Middle School, the current place of worship for New Zion Christian Fellowship. Michael had stayed home, choosing to pack up the camping gear instead of go to church, which seemed hypocritical since he had been so quick to condemn me.

Upon entering the school cafeteria, which served as the sanctuary for Sunday services, I was handed a bulletin and pulled into the warm embrace of one of the greeters. A podium, an overhead projector, and an area set up with audio equipment and instruments for the worship team sat at the front of the cafeteria, while rows of chairs lined the floor, surrounded by lunch tables. We inconspicuously slid into the back row.

Friendly conversations filled the room, with many people sharing what God had done in their lives during the week. The man at the microphone opened with prayer, then worship began as guitars and a keyboard played a song of praise. We sang the lyrics that were projected on the wall, proclaiming the power of Jesus. Amid the sounds of tambourines and clapping, some danced at their seats while others took to the aisles in joyful celebration. Others stood still or raised their hands in quieter form of worship. It seemed like everyone except me was actively participating.

My focus was on the end of the service, and the worship seemed to go on forever. In times past I would have slipped into my ballet slippers and joined the women in the back of the church in an improvisational dance as an expression of worship. Now I no longer felt His presence, and that made me angry. Like a jilted lover, I battled rejection and hurt, allowing myself to withdraw even further from my relationship with God.

My daughter Missy made her way over to Pastor John, or "Uncle John" as she called him. She tugged at his pant leg and waited for him to look down and smile. When he reached down, she gave him the biggest hug she possibly could. Then after whispering a few words to her, Pastor John sent her on her way back to me.

Finally, the music quieted and the singing changed from the song on the overhead to the utterance of voices in a harmonious wave rising and falling in volume—singing in the Spirit, as it was called. I found myself thinking that it wouldn't be too much longer now. I knew the familiar Sunday routine. Next, the overhead would be shut off and the lights would be turned back on as all silently waited for the prophets— mouthpieces of God—to share revelations with the church body.

I looked at my watch, impatiently waiting for the children to be dismissed to Sunday school. My children didn't need me to walk them to their classrooms, as they would have readily gone with the other children, but I had another reason for taking them.

Once they were in their classrooms, I made my way to the bathroom and allowed enough time to pass so that I would miss communion. I knew the things I had become involved with weren't godly and that the Bible warned against partaking of the bread and the wine in an unworthy manner. Until I had things straight in my head, I didn't want to take the chance of bringing sickness on myself by not heeding this Scripture. Skipping out with the children provided a way to get out of communion without being confronted week after week as I passed the bread and cup without partaking.

Once I thought I had waited long enough, I quietly opened the bathroom door and listened for the teaching to begin. I then slipped into my chair in the back of the room, contemplating why I had even bothered to come. It was becoming increasingly more difficult to keep my attention focused on what was being taught.

Finally, the hour-long teaching came to a close with prayer. I gathered my belongings, anxious to get the kids, hurry home, change into something more comfortable, and go outside to enjoy the beauty of the day.

A WITCH'S ENCOUNTER WITH GOD

CHAPTER FOUR

—ᵚᵚᵚ—

It was barely dawn when I finished showering. This was the only hour I could find for total relaxation without being interrupted. I locked the bathroom door, threw on my soft white cotton robe, and finished drying my hair. Then reaching into the cabinet, I retrieved the sea salt and drew a perfect clockwise circle of protection around myself. I dropped my robe to the floor as I visualized a transparent white shield surrounding me and extending well into the universe. Waiting patiently, I allowed my mind to drift into a trance-like state.

The familiar presence of my spirit guide soon materialized, breathing over my shoulder. This higher entity planted the word *transformation* within me, and I thanked her for the message I received and then drew a deep breath, releasing the energy that encompassed me. I asked for a blessing, and as the white protective shield dissipated, I felt strong and powerful.

—ᵚᵚᵚ—

I felt the same chill up my spine that I had experienced many years before. How could I forget that day when, fresh out of high school, I first heard the song that mesmerized me with its haunting vocals? The enchanting lyrics told the story of a Welsh goddess and soon became one of my favorite songs, until I became a Christian and the church persuaded me to forsake all music that didn't glorify God.

This time, the chill came as I read the story that unfolded before me. She appeared, accompanied by magical birds whose captivating songs could awaken the dead and lure the living to sleep. I was drawn to her, Rhiannon of the Birds, the otherworldly lunar goddess of inspiration. This was the goddess I would personally begin working with. I closed the book, *The Mabinogion.* I would get back to it later, but for now I had to get back to the bus.

—m—

The cage, perch, and treats were already on the pet store counter as we checked out the new hatchlings in the incubator. They were bald little critters with big bulging eyes and a crop that was half the size of the bird.

"Look how wide he opens his mouth," Lynn said, amazed as the chick opened its beak waiting to be fed.

"They look kind of ugly if you ask me," Aaron added.

Peering at the helpless chick, I agreed, "Definitely an ugly duckling, but look how beautiful they become." I motioned for the kids to follow me to the cages that held the lovely young birds.

Since the handfed babies were a pricey purchase, the young ones were the way to go. I looked in through the cage bars and saw her, a Lutino cockatiel. Her plumage was as white as snow, accented by her yellow face, crest, and cheeks. The sales clerk took her out and wrapped her in a towel, then handed her to me. I already sensed the magical connection between us and knew this dear feathered friend would aid in my spellwork.

Michael met us at the cashier and bought her as my birthday gift. I was surprised but thrilled that Michael was smiling and gave me a birthday hug, acting more like the man I first married. We got in the car and headed home.

"What are we going to call her?" Missy asked.

I'd already decided. "Her name is Luna."

"Where are we going to keep her?" Aaron asked.

"She'll be staying in my room."

The kids squawked, hoping I'd change my mind, but I wasn't about to reconsider. Luna wasn't a family pet, but my magical companion.

—∿—

The emotional temperature inside our home matched the falling temperatures outside as winter approached. Trees had long since dropped their leaves, leaving them bare and mysterious in the moonlight. Wrapped in my black velvet cape, I stood outside taking in all the beauty around me and enjoying how peaceful it was without the noise of the television and the ever-increasing tension inside.

Michael made his unhappiness known by stomping through the house, and it sounded like a herd of elephants every time he came down the stairs. He seemed angry at the world. My soul longed for so much more than what my current life offered, and with Christmas fast approaching, I felt even more confusion and unrest.

Christmastime had once been my favorite time of the year, as I looked forward to the festive glow about every home and the joyful songs that could be heard everywhere, but this year I was unsure how to handle it. We had always gone to church to celebrate Jesus' birth. If I didn't go, it would certainly raise questions—yet how could I go on pretending to be a Christian when I was treading a path of magic? This would be my first Christmas without Jesus, and even though I had no interest in celebrating, would it be fair to deny my kids the thrill of waking up on Christmas morning to an assortment of gifts beneath the Christmas tree?

A thought then occurred to me. From a Christian point of view, the true meaning of Christmas was distorted by stories of a red-suited Santa sliding down chimneys, filling stockings, and leaving gifts under the tree. For the first time, I could allow my children to experience Santa without feeling guilty. This would be a new adventure for them, and I again began to look forward to the holiday season after all.

Having settled what to do about Christmas for the children, I began reading the next lesson in my witchcraft course. Ironically, it covered the different Sabbats celebrated by those in the Craft. I was delighted to find that the next one was on December twenty-first. Not only was it the Winter Solstice, the longest night of the year, but it was also the rebirth of the Sun God. As I read further, I realized I had something to celebrate after all. I wrote down everything I would need to celebrate the Winter Solstice, or Yule as it was more commonly called.

The phone rang and I answered it, still distracted by thoughts of my Yuletide celebration.

"Hey, my gal, are you coming to the Christmas dinner?" Pastor John asked.

Caught off guard, I fumbled for a valid reason for not attending.

"Um ... Well, I don't think we'll make it this year. We can't really afford to go."

"Money's not a problem," he insisted. "I'd hate for you to miss out on some good food and fellowship."

"Honestly, John, it's more than food or fellowship. It's about God being distant." Then I blurted out, "Why would I want to celebrate His birth when He abandoned me?"

Pastor John spoke calmly. "God has not and never will abandon you. He has promised He will never leave you nor forsake you. There are times we may not think He's there, but He is. Maybe you don't feel His presence right now, but that doesn't mean He isn't there."

I had always sought and taken Pastor John's advice—always listened to what he had to say and believed he had my best interest in mind. But this time I knew God was not in my life and Pastor John could not convince me otherwise. Feeling this whole conversation had merely confirmed everything I had been thinking about Christmas, I preceded with my plans for celebrating the Winter Solstice.

—ɷ—

On December twenty-first, I gathered my children together and ventured out into the woods behind our house to search for the things I had written on my Yule celebration list. We found wild ivy, a branch from a holly tree, a pine cone, a few oak nuts, and a beautiful white birch tree log. Under the guise of our "fun family outing," we headed back home and carefully laid everything on the dining room table. I fixed the kids some hot cocoa and began assembling my Yule log.

The birch tree log was cut to a good size, allowing enough space to drill three holes for the symbolic candles I had purchased earlier. My family would never know that the three-candle centerpiece was anything more than a homemade holiday decoration. I arranged a few sprigs of pine from the Christmas tree around the log, then added the ivy, holly, pine cones, and nuts. A perfect Yule log!

By now the sun had set, so I carried the Yule log into the living room, placed it on top of the entertainment center, and lit one candle at a time. No one heard the silent prayers I sent to the God and the Goddess for the light the Winter Solstice would bring.

—ɷ—

Christmas Eve arrived, and we carried on with our tradition of going to church. Even Michael joined us. The service began with the traditional Christmas hymns, and the sermon was relatively short, giving ample time for families to get home and finish up their Christmas Eve traditions.

Several members of New Zion came by later with so many gifts for the children that all the space beneath our tree was full. I sat in amazement as the lights on the tree revealed that the stockings hung on the stairwell were also stuffed with holiday goodies. Considering my spiritual mind-set, I felt guilty taking the gifts, but I accepted their generosity for the sake of the children.

CHAPTER FIVE

—ɯ—

S now was in the forecast, and the howling cold wind made it a perfect time to stay busy indoors. Part of my next lesson consisted of assembling my own sacred tools and making my ritual robe. I had shopped extensively to find the right material—black and 100 percent cotton—and was quite amazed that I remembered enough from my junior high sewing class to make my own robe. I chose black since it was a combination of all colors and I already had a white one that I had been using for meditation. Finding the appropriate rope to use as my cord had proved a little more challenging, as it seemed everything was now made from a polyester blend, but after a long search, I found the cotton cord I needed.

To be less conspicuous, I found an old wooden-handled knife—a hand-me-down from my grandmother—to use as my athame, or ritual knife. I placed it in a bowl with sea salt and water to cleanse it from any negativity as I repeated, "I cleanse this blade of steel and purify it from all negativity, that it might aid me in my workings. By the power of the elements, you are cleansed."

After anointing it with water, I sprinkled it with salt and passed it through incense smoke, focusing on the knife being blessed while repeating, "I bless and consecrate this athame that it might aid me in my workings. By the powers of the Lord and Lady, you are consecrated." Lastly, I opened the window and placed it on the window ledge in the direct full moonlight, allowing it to absorb the power from the moon overnight.

The following night, I removed it from the window ledge and, holding it in my dominant hand, visualized my energy entering the athame. I then charged it by saying, "I charge you by the Lord and Lady, by the powers of air, fire, water, and earth, be charged, creature of life."

For an altar, I chose an old round table handed down from my great-aunt. I draped a white cloth over it and positioned two candleholders—one with a silver candle to represent the Goddess on one side and one with a gold candle to represent the God on the other. In the center went my small crystal ball accompanied by my incense burner, which was in the shape of a mini cauldron.

I had to be quite careful about what I allowed to be visible, so I carefully concealed my personal "Book of Shadows," which contained spells and rituals I had either done or collected in my studies, as well as incantations to the God and the Goddess and a list of magical uses for herbs and stones.

—∽—

Since Michael hadn't mentioned anything about my new spirituality in weeks, I thought I had been successfully discreet with my preparations—until I arrived home after shopping and went into the playroom to see the kids. I stepped over Barbie dolls and Hot Wheels scattered about, but not one of them got up to come to me. In fact, they huddled closer together and didn't even look up. When I asked what was wrong, I received a response I'd never dreamt I would get.

"Daddy said we need to be careful of you because you're spiritually sick," Lynn said, caressing her stuffed glow worm.

"What does spiritually sick mean, Mommy?" Missy asked timidly.

I couldn't believe my ears! This was the most ridiculous thing I'd ever heard. How dare he!

"Daddy is wrong. I'm not sick," I reassured them. "And I will straighten this matter out right now."

I angrily went looking for Michael, only to find him consumed in a book. My fury released as I confronted him, "What's this about me being spiritually sick?"

He looked up. "You're not thinking right, and Pastor John agreed we needed to let the children know that you're not following godly ways."

"Telling them I'm not following godly ways is one thing," I snapped. "But telling them I'm sick is something I will not tolerate, and I intend to call Pastor John this very minute."

Before Michael could say another word, I grabbed the phone, determined to get this straightened out right away. I couldn't reach him though, so I stomped out of the room in frustration.

I spent the rest of the evening with my children, reassuring them I was fine. The rage I felt couldn't even be put into words. I felt betrayed by a father figure and my own husband, caught between wanting to scream in anger or cry out in pain. While I could understand their disapproval of my lifestyle, why had they taken such extreme measures? Had they even considered the impact of their actions on the children?

I vowed that I would take care of it tomorrow as soon as I got home from work. They would not be allowed to bring the children into what should be left to adult discussion.

The next morning after my morning runs, I hurried home and headed straight for the phone. Pastor John answered right away, and I got right to the point. "Michael told the children that I'm spiritually sick because I've chosen another path, and he said you were the one who suggested it!"

"You're deceived right now, my dear," he said with disappointment in his voice. "This other path you're getting involved with is witchcraft—something that will hurt you and your children."

Shocked by his accusation, I fought to keep from screaming

at him. "I'm not deceived. It's true I no longer see things as you do, but tell me how I have hurt my children by studying about Wicca?"

His next words nearly pushed me past the point of self-control: "You're caught in a lie straight from hell, and Satan would have you believe it's all innocent. But you need to be made aware of what happens to children in the hands of Satanists."

I was furious. How dare he make such statements without knowing what he was talking about!

"First of all, this is Wicca, not something satanic," I said. "Our belief is to harm no one. Wiccans believe all life is sacred, even the plants and trees. Wiccans don't believe there is a Satan, except maybe in the minds of Christians. You don't even know anything about it, yet you so easily condemn it."

"I may not know all the details of Wicca," he replied, "but I do know the Bible says 'thou shalt not have any gods before me.' Who do you think the god of witchcraft is? In the spiritual realm, you're dealing with God, with angels, or with demons."

Obviously he was totally uninformed, but I decided to get back to the topic that was really at hand. "Tell me what have you seen in me. Show me one thing I have said or done that would suggest my children are potentially in harm's way."

The momentary silence on the other end of the line confirmed I had hit home.

"Well, there isn't anything you have done," he slowly confirmed, "and I know how much you love your children. It's just that we are concerned about what this could lead to."

Feeling I had nearly won the battle, I declared, "Well, maybe you should get your facts straight before upsetting my children, especially when I've done nothing to warrant your accusations."

When he said, "This was not intended to upset the children," I knew I had turned the tide.

After that, it didn't take long to convince Pastor John to speak to Michael. When Michael came home from work that night, he told me he had already talked to Pastor John and agreed to have a talk with the kids. But when bedtime arrived and he still hadn't dealt with the issue, I determined that the children shouldn't have to go to bed another night with such worry hanging over them.

After their bubble baths, the kids all headed upstairs to the girls' room for a bedtime story. They shared half a room that was divided by a staircase. At the top of the staircase was a Polly Pocket clock in the shape of a wristwatch against the pink wall. I walked across the soft green carpet and sat down on Lynn's bed. The kids cuddled next to me with the bubblegum scent still lingering from their baths. I opened the book and began reading.

Michael came in to say good-night while we were finishing the story, and I took the opportunity and told them that their daddy had something important to tell them.

Lynn got up on her knees, nervously biting her nails. Missy's eyes were as wide as walnuts, and Aaron stopped making his motor sounds to hear what his dad had to say.

With all eyes on him, Michael sat down with a huff and told the children it was all a misunderstanding—that Mommy wasn't sick just because she had chosen not to follow Jesus.

Lynn's dimples filled her rosy cheeks, and Missy jumped up and down on the bed as Aaron wrapped his arms around my neck. After kissing and then tucking each of the children into bed, I said good-night and then went to the bedroom while Michael headed downstairs.

But the sense of relief I felt now that the children had been told the truth was marred by the fact that Michael and Pastor John had conspired against me. If they had gone so far as to involve the children, how far would they ultimately go to interfere with my further studies?

I thought about the things I had shared in confidence with Pastor John concerning my relationship with Michael. Had they truly remained confidential? Even though my trust in him was shaken, I didn't want to completely stop talking to Pastor John.

But if I wanted to continue on my own path of discovery, something had to be done to stop him and Michael from scheming behind my back. I couldn't risk the welfare of the children to their combined acts of religious paranoia.

Still, I had come far enough in my studies to see a solution to my problem and a harmless way to keep them from hindering my journey on this new path. I went through my drawer and choose a black votive candle, then approached my altar and placed it in the center. After lighting the candle, I visualized Michael and Pastor John distant and not speaking with one another. I saw myself protected and free to continue growing in the old ways. I continued this imagery in a meditative state until the candle burned down, then pinched the flame out and visualized the energy being sent forth into the universe to bring my desired result.

CHAPTER SIX

—⁂—

I sat sipping my morning coffee and glancing through the *Daily News* when a photo of a man and woman dressed in black seemed to jump off the page. They stood behind a counter with what looked like crystals hanging in the background. The heading read, "Witches Going Green."

I couldn't believe my eyes, and quickly read through the article featuring a local witch shop that was promoting Earth Day. I had been working pretty much solitary (alone) but had begun to desire contact with others of a like mind so I could eventually become part of a coven. My initial excitement then turned to panic when I realized the shop was closing. I needed to investigate immediately.

My friend Tiffany agreed to babysit for me at the last minute. She had a daughter the same age as one of mine and we attended the same church. I dropped the kids off, thanked her for her help, and hurried out the door. On the ride there, I hoped my old car would make the trip. I was also a bit apprehensive about meeting other witches for the first time.

I followed the directions scribbled on a used envelope, making the twenty-five-minute drive to the shopping center where the store was located. As I got out and walked toward the small witch shop, I felt like a fugitive making my way to freedom. With no familiar faces around me, I quickly entered the store.

To my left were showcases filled with candles, runes, tarot cards, and athames. On the right sat an altar arrayed for magical working. I made my way to the back, where a rather tall man was looking through a wide selection of books, and recognized the couple from the newspaper standing behind the counter.

Suddenly, the store lit up with bright light and a voice behind me said, "We're live here at Cerridwen's Cauldron."

Stunned, I spun around to find myself staring into a large television camera lens. I quickly turned back to the books, looking for a place to hide. The only way out was behind the camera. My heart raced as I repetitively projected the thought, *I can't be seen on TV.*

The camera crew rehearsed their introduction three times before heading outside to film some witches picking up litter from the streets. I grabbed a book on the magical uses of herbs and took it to the counter to buy it. Conan, the man at the register, gave me a business card and information for their mail-order catalog. Careful to avoid the TV camera, I quickly left the store.

As I drove home, panic hit me. How could I possibly explain what I was doing in a witch shop after dropping my children off at a Christian friend's house? What if Pastor John got word of it? I formulated a list of options, and by the time I picked up the kids, I had a plan. When we arrived home, I rushed into the house and called my sister, Melinda, then asked her to watch and record the six o'clock news for me. This way I would know what anyone from church might have seen of me at the shop.

As I prepared dinner, I made sure our television was on a different channel and hoped Michael would follow his normal after-dinner routine. Six o'clock came and went, and Michael went into seclusion in our bedroom with a book in hand. I waited impatiently for Melinda to call and tell me how well she could see me.

To my amazement, she watched the report on the store and saw some guy looking at books, but there was no sign of me. *Impossible*, I thought. I had looked right at the camera. I had to be there! At the same time, I was thrilled that I hadn't shown up on the report. Still, I wanted to see it for myself, so I told Michael and the kids that I needed to run over to my sister's house.

Melinda had already rewound the videotape for me, so all I

had to do was hit the *play* button. As I watched, the front view of the shop came into view. Then the camera zoomed inside, right over to the wall with the bookshelf. The tall guy I had been standing next to was there looking at the books, but I wasn't.

After several replays of the tape, I realized everything had happened just as I had experienced it, but I was missing. Had my thoughts of the danger of being seen on prime-time news released energies that made me invisible? Was there protection from another source that kept me hidden from view while the news was broadcast? I wasn't sure, but whatever happened, it worked and I was not on the news.

A week went by, and no one mentioned my adventure to the witch shop. Feeling it was safe to pursue this new resource, I fumbled through my pocketbook and found the shop's phone number. A recording told me how to send for a catalog. Until now, all my tools had been handmade. While that had been rewarding and added my own energy to the tool at hand, it would be good to buy some of the things that were harder to make. They also carried herbs, so I could now purchase the ones I couldn't grow in my own garden.

—⚭—

Though I felt the thrill of a child discovering something for the first time, I was also torn as I watched my church family begin to distance themselves from me. I could understand them not agreeing with my new outlook on spirituality, but I couldn't understand how they could claim to love me yet choose to separate from me just because I no longer shared the same belief. To me, it seemed that friendship should be able to withstand a difference in a point of view.

A feeling of guilt overcame me when I missed church again, so I called Pastor Jacob and his wife, Liz, whom I considered good friends. They were sort of an odd couple—Pastor Jacob was a rather large man with a beard and longish hair while Liz was petite with a quiet spirit and was an accomplished seamstress.

He played the piano and was part of the music ministry in the church, and she and I had children around the same age and had been part of a young mother's group.

Pastor Jacob knew of my struggles with Christianity, so I didn't hesitate to call him. The call started out friendly enough, but he became quite annoyed when the conversation shifted to my current spiritual state of mind. Before I knew it, we were engaged in more of a heated debate. Then he said the words I feared: "If this is how you feel, then you're in a backslidden state and have given yourself and your family over to the hands of the enemy. In the best interest of our church family, you cannot be permitted to come to church anymore until you repent."

I wasn't ready to turn my back on Christianity altogether, so I tried to reason with him. "No, please, Jacob, this is not good. I did everything the church told me to do and now we're paying the price. Why is it when I submitted to Michael's authority, we became victims of his bad choices? And what about God's promises that never happened in my poverty-stricken household? Can you explain why God abandoned me when I desperately cried for help? And now you so easily close the door. Don't you think this will only further my unbelief?"

"That it may," he said, "but we cannot jeopardize the other people in the church while you dabble in witchcraft!"

Still not willing to give up, I countered, "But didn't Jesus come for the lost and the sinners?"

"The Bible clearly states to suffer the witch not even to live."

Wondering how the conversation had become so angry, I asked, "Doesn't the Bible also say to love your neighbor as yourself? So what do you do if your neighbor is a witch?"

Suddenly, I was given a glimpse into the spiritual realm. It took a few seconds to adjust to the blinding light allowing me to make out their translucent human form. Angels! I stood speechless, captivated by their countenance. I sensed the angels were attempting to calm the fury within Pastor Jacob but were intercepted by the daunting presence of their shadowy counterparts, who were similar in form but void of the inner light leaving them dull like smoky quartz.

"Ally, did you hear me?" he asked. "I said, I suggest you get out your Bible and read about what God has to say about witchcraft. In the meantime, you are not to come back."

"Jacob, please, no. Don't do this," I pleaded, trying to regain my composure.

"There's no reason to continue going on about this. I'll talk to Pastor John, but I can assure you he is in agreement with me."

Had the shadows actually coerced Jacob into believing he was doing the work of God by excommunicating me from the church? I sat there in disbelief, wrestling with the vision I had experienced. Pastor Jacob was a discerning man, so why hadn't he seen what was happening in the Spirit?

I felt troubled and angry that Pastor Jacob would excommunicate me, knowing the struggle I was having. I called Pastor John, but my dialogue with him went pretty much the same as the one with Pastor Jacob. He reminded me of Matthew 18, which states if a brother refuses to listen even to the church, then he is to be treated as a pagan or a tax collector. I then told him about the vision and how it seemed I was backstage watching this dramatic scene unfold.

"The way to determine if something is of God is to see how it lines up with His Word," Pastor John advised me. "Since Matthew 18 is scriptural, then what you experienced must have come from another source ... and we know who that is."

He was gentler in his explanation of their actions, saying this was to be a form of discipline with the intention of restoring me back into a relationship with God. When I asked how keeping me away would draw me back, he only said, "I'll discuss this with Pastor Jacob, but in the meantime, you shouldn't question the word of God."

Being banished from church was like having your own father insist that you weren't allowed at home anymore unless you believed as he did. I felt deeply hurt as I hung up the phone. Others had been asked to leave the church at times, always with the ultimate hope that they would come to their senses and get their life right with God, but I'd never dreamt it would happen to me. And I couldn't remember anyone who had returned.

I researched what people did in biblical times when someone was removed from fellowship. It most likely meant that they were sent to the edge of town without any communication with anyone and with no food or drink. Once the banished person got hungry and thirsty enough, they would be ready to do whatever was needed to get back into the fellowship, but I didn't see how that kind of logic would work today. In fact, this would likely have the opposite effect, giving me another reason to find fellowship with others of a like mind. Ironically, it seemed that more would be accomplished by drawing someone in than pushing them away. After all, wasn't that what the Bible taught?

Those next few days seemed endless as I waited for Pastor John's decision regarding my fate. Hopefully, after some prayer, he would reconsider (I still believed he would ultimately be in my corner and would never agree with excommunicating me).

The phone call came midweek. Once the small talk was out of the way, Pastor John informed me, "Pastor Jacob spoke with me, concerned over your dabbling in witchcraft. The eldership discussed this at length, and we've decided that unless you denounce witchcraft and turn back to God, you will no longer be permitted to attend church."

I almost dropped the phone as I put my hand over the mouthpiece for fear of what I might say.

He continued, "You're associating with demons, Ally. What you really need right now is deliverance from their influence. You know we love you and your family, but until you decide who you will serve, we have no alternative but to apply Matthew 18."

I felt the blood rush to my face and my blood pressure rise. "Matthew 18? So, what, you're kicking me out?" Who did they think they were, deciding who could go to church?

"We're not kicking you out. You just have to get right with God before you can come back." Pastor John then finished, "We'll be praying for you."

I lost it. Half crying and half yelling into the phone, I said, "That's the same as kicking me out. Aren't you supposed be to drawing people in instead of kicking them out? How can you do this? Never mind, forget it!" I slammed the phone down, hanging up on him.

Wasn't God's love unconditional? Didn't His Word say He loves the sinner just as much as the saint? Where was God in all this? I reflected on the day when I called out to Him in desperation, and thought about how I had obtained the strength to overcome. All this time I had been rebuilding the very foundation that I stood on. These were major turning points in my life, and I had come too far to turn back now.

The following Sunday, Pastor John made a statement to the congregation on my spiritual state, asking the body of believers to pray for me but refrain from any contact until I choose to repent. Pam, one of the two women from church whom I considered close friends, called me afterward. He had pulled both her and Tiffany aside privately and requested that they not associate with me. Pam told me she was going to abide by Pastor John's advice and would be out of contact. While I strongly disagreed with their whole approach, I respected her for being upfront and honest.

Tiffany was another matter. I called her, but she refused to answer any of my calls. I left several messages on her answering machine, all of which she ignored. When her young children answered the phone, which I found unusual, they said their mother wasn't there and apparently neither was their dad or a babysitter, so I knew Tiffany was ignoring my calls.

I finally drove to her house and knocked on the door. Her daughter answered and said she'd get her mom. So I waited, fidgeting with my car keys for what seemed like a half hour before Tiffany finally came out. I cut to the chase: "I know Pastor John made an announcement in church to dis-fellowship with me, but since we're good friends, I want to know if you plan on following his advice."

She looked like a deer in headlights, caught by a question she hadn't expected. "I heard what Pastor John said, but we're still friends. Nothing has changed on my end."

I didn't believe her, but knew I couldn't force honesty out of her. "Are you sure you're okay with us remaining friends? Because I know your kids weren't home alone, and you've never returned my calls."

She stared at the cement sidewalk. "I've just been really busy lately."

I walked to my car, but before getting in, I turned around. "If everything is really okay, I'm sure I will be hearing from you shortly."

With no response, Tiffany opened the door and went back inside. I never heard from her again.

—⟋⟍—

About a month later I called Pastor Jacob's wife, Liz, asking when I could return a few books that belonged to her. Surprisingly, she said she had to check with Pastor Jacob first to see when he would be home. I hung up wondering why it had to be so complicated. A few days later, I received a call letting me know an appropriate time.

As I approached their back door, I saw Liz look out the window, but it was Pastor Jacob who answered the door. I immediately knew that he was exhibiting his spiritual covering, or spiritual protection, over his wife. Our church believed that a woman should be under her husband's spiritual "covering" and, if she operated outside of that covering, she likely would fall victim to the enemy's attack. It was as though I was the devil himself coming on the attack.

I was rather annoyed. After all the years they had known me, they should've known better.

Pastor Jacob didn't invite me inside, but we ended up having a good discussion standing on the porch. He gave me an opportunity to explain where I was coming from. What looked like genuine sorrow filled his eyes as he said, "It's not that we want to do this, but your decision to continue being involved in witchcraft leaves us no other choice."

With him seeming more compassionate, I tried to plead my case one more time. "I don't expect you to encourage my involvement, nor do I expect you to agree. I respect your stand on your biblical point of view, but to say I can't come to church doesn't make sense. I would think it would be all the more reason you'd be telling me to come. The church is like family to me. How would you feel if your family told you they didn't want you around anymore just because you had a different point of view?"

"It's not like that," he said, "but you're right. You do need Jesus in your life. You can come here on Thursday nights for prayer meeting, and if you have any questions about what the Bible says, we can talk about that as well."

Surprised, I asked, "Won't that cause controversy with the eldership after they kicked me out?"

He shook his head. "Nobody kicked you out, and no, it's not going to present a problem. You're welcome in my home for prayer meetings."

"Thanks, Jacob." I walked back to my car.

I was straddling the fence between Christianity and Wicca, not completely letting go of one or embracing the other. I had heard stories at New Zion about people who left and then suffered horrible accidents as a result of being out from under the church's spiritual covering, so the thought of completely walking away terrified me. They had been told that if they chose to leave, they would be vulnerable to enemy attack and even divine retribution. At the same time, I still had some apprehension about the unknown territory of Wicca, so I wasn't ready to close either door.

CbAPTER SEVEN

—ᴍᴧ—

M ichael hurried in the door carrying a metal box and cleared the coffee table of magazines and books with one swipe of his arm. Cujo, right by his side, sniffed around it like a hound dog fresh on its trail. Michael patted Cujo's head as he glanced over at me, looking like a kid in a candy store. "Come here and take a look at this."

I still didn't know what to make of it. "Just a sec. I have to check on dinner."

As I turned to go to the kitchen, he unplugged the television. What had gotten into him? He had a glimmer in his eye that reminded me of our first date.

I opened the oven door and checked the chicken, then seeing it still had a way to go, put the timer back on and hurried back to check out his mysterious box. It contained a mini screen and keyboard. As we explored a whole new world—cyberspace—I stared with childlike wonder.

I knew nothing about internet service, but it didn't take long for me to discover how to navigate it. Michael's enthusiasm was contagious as he helped me locate the music message boards. He had come a long way since laying down the law regarding rock music, and I attributed that to the spell I'd cast to keep him and Pastor John from speaking.

We had dinner in the living room that night, which the kids thought was a great idea. It was almost like old times until Michael just got up and withdrew upstairs, leaving us behind. Now that I had the computer all to myself, I found an entire board dedicated to my favorite artist. Fans from all over the country shared about a new release, the latest rumors, and how they were touched by her music. I added my thoughts to the message board and soon had several responses. This was so cool!

After several notes back and forth, I found a friend who shared a mutual interest in music. We had an immediate connection, as if we were long-lost friends. As we emailed back and forth, I found out his name was Bo and he lived with his wife, Desiree, clear across the country. We had a lot in common, and for a second I had the strange feeling that he might be the soul mate I asked for in what I thought was an unanswered spell.

Several months before, I had stood before my altar and lit the pink and white candles that were anointed with lavender oil. Petals were scattered about the altar top, adding the scent of roses to that of the incense smoke twirling upward. I concentrated on the words as I spoke, "Goddess of love, send my soul mate, the one meant just for me. He's searching somewhere, and I for he. Thank you, Goddess, for sending my love to me."

Looking back to the email on my screen, I remembered that Bo was married, so I quickly dismissed the idea. Still, before long we were conversing on a daily basis. This was something I could put my time and energy into instead of dwelling on the recent rejection by my church family.

Now I could hardly wait for Michael to come home each night so I could use the computer and check in with my new cyber friends. I had met so many interesting people and connected with others with a common interest, unaware of how hungry I'd been for fellowship.

Curious to see what other message boards were out there, I found a religion message board and even a section on Wicca. A lot of other people shared the same belief, and I began connecting with those of a like mind through the message board. Tons of information on magic, spells, and rituals were downloaded and printed for future reference. This was opening a whole new world I never knew existed.

I met Cora on the Wicca message board. She was a mature woman of Irish descent and had just discovered Wicca. We felt an immediate connection and discovered we lived only about an hour from one another. After some discussion, we met at a shopping village, halfway between the two of us, that was known for its diversity and eclectic people. It contained several witch-related shops we could visit, and she also told me about a new shop that sounded like the shop I had visited a year ago.

The drive was a pleasant one, with a rushing river on one side and mountains on the other. I passed a sign that read *Danger, Falling Rocks*, and looked up at the mountainside as I cautiously crossed over the steel grates of the bridge over the river. Once in the quaint town, I parked, donned my black cape, and proceeded to our designated meeting spot.

Soon a short, fair, red-haired woman wrapped in an Irish wool cape approached. We greeted each other and then walked the shop-lined streets until the scent of incense paved the way to a door with a wicker pentagram on it. The sign on the window read *Cerridwen's Cauldron*. We ended up talking for hours with the shop owners, and before long it was nightfall and time to make our purchases and head home.

"Blessed be and come again," Conan said as we were walking out the door.

"Blessed be," we replied in unison.

We walked back to the place we met, then exchanged a warm embrace before going our separate ways, saying, "It's merry to have met you."

—ɷ—

At home, my marriage continued to deteriorate. The kids and I had just finished another meal in the absence of their father.

Michael no longer joined us at the dinner table. Each night he grabbed his plate and headed upstairs to eat in front of his newest makeshift computer, composed of leftover parts from his job.

After I finished the dishes, I went upstairs to tell him about a new online provider I had heard about. His eyes were fixed on the nude blonde on the screen in front of him.

He quickly closed the screen, annoyed at my intrusion. I really didn't mind the nudity as much as his lack of interest in me. As a matter of fact, it seemed he had now lost interest in the entire household except for his daily dose of eye candy. The bathtub drain was emptying into the basement with each shower, and he hadn't bothered to fix it. Every time it rained, the kitchen roof leaked, and I couldn't understand his lack of concern over the kids' safety.

Michael didn't react to my telling him about the new online option. In fact, I could have been a fly on the wall and received more of a response. He had some nerve telling me I was spiritually sick when he was the one with the zombie-like stare and a Fort Knox shell that prevented anyone from reaching him. What confused me was that other times he would be himself, playing with the children or talking about work. Even then, the lack of intimacy between us remained. It was more than feeling sexually deprived; what I really missed and wanted was his love and attention.

At least Michael wasn't harping on me about spiritual beliefs any more. In fact, he had taken the official title of—as my dad would say—a C&E Christian: Christmas and Easter only. Pastor John no longer came over for what had been weekly counseling sessions. During the last one, Michael had barricaded himself in our bedroom, refusing to come down to negotiate our relationship. I felt a bit responsible, convinced that the spell I had done was the cause of their dissension.

Pastor John wasn't the only one Michael had disassociated himself with. It was tradition for the family to have Sunday dinner at my parents' home. We always had a full-course meal consisting of roast and potatoes, something we could never afford at home. Around two p.m. I called for the kids, who came running knowing they were going to their grandparents, but Michael remained upstairs. When he didn't respond, I went up to find him lying across the bed face down.

I nudged him. "Wake up. It's time to go to my mom's."

Michael half-heartily mumbled that he was staying home because he was tired.

I went downstairs and got in the car with the kids, then drove to my parents' house and arrived to find dinner being placed on the table.

"Where's Michael?" my dad asked.

"Oh, he's home resting," I replied.

My dad didn't say anything further, but I knew what he was thinking. Michael hadn't been to a Sunday family dinner now in months, and his lame excuse wasn't working any more.

A WITCH'S ENCOUNTER WITH ÇOD

CHAPTER EIGHT

—⚭—

It was nearing midnight as I finished bathing in a tub with sea salt and narcissus oil. After drying off, I slipped my white robe on and grabbed my basket of supplies before heading outside in my yard. I placed a white candle on an outdoor table and turned my Book of Shadows to the handwritten dedication.

Beneath the thin crescent of a waxing moon, I visualized being encircled by white light energy. I took a deep breath, calming my heart while I concentrated on the elements around me. The sound of the neighbor's waterfall trickling and the cool night air on my moist skin made me quiver as I stared into the dancing candle flame and felt the cool dry earth beneath my feet.

"Mother Goddess, Father God, I open myself to your presence and dedicate myself to you and the old ways." I took the vial of oil and anointed my forehead, continuing, "May my mind be blessed, so that I can understand the wisdom of the gods." Then I gently anointed my eyelids. "May my eyes be blessed, so I can clearly see my way upon thy path." I touched my lips with the oil. "May my lips be blessed, that I may speak thy ways discreetly."

Anointing my hands, I went on, "May my hands be blessed, so they may heal others." I opened my robe in the moonlight, then anointed the skin of my chest, covered in goose bumps. "May my heart be blessed, so I may love and be loved." I anointed my genital area. "May my womb be blessed, that I may bring forth life, the ultimate gift of your love and sacred union."

Lastly, I anointed the soles of my feet. "May my feet be blessed, so that I may walk the path of magic with the divine."

After taking a deep breath, I proclaimed, "I now belong to the Craft and embrace it with all that it entails in perfect love and in perfect trust. So mote it be."

That was the turning point in my life. Besides having a good foundation on the history and the basics of the Craft, I now was a Dedicant, making my choice to walk, learn, and grow in the Goddess's ways of magic. While I was being guided by the high priest of the school, I was working solitary for the most part. Being a solitary had its advantages, but I still desired the coven experience. A whole magical world waited to be explored, and this was only the beginning.

Before climbing into bed that night, I walked over to Luna, who was hanging on the bars of her cage anticipating my goodnight kiss. After a quick peck, she retreated to her perch and I covered her cage for the night. I slid beneath the covers of the bed, making every attempt not to disturb Michael's sound sleep. The faint scent of narcissus lingered as I fell into a deep slumber.

In a dream, I was led into a splendidly green meadow. Rocky hills crossed the horizon, outstretched for miles, and before me were the throne of the Goddess and an assembly of immortals. Instantly I was strolling through a courtyard among ancient stone castles, searching for an esoteric treasure. The journey took me to a village where the chatter of commoners was heard. At the edge of town was a forest.

The enchanting sight of the Goddess enthralled me as she offered me a bronze cauldron. Before leaving me at the threshold of the forest, she said, "Daughter, here the secret lies. Take the cauldron and learn to be wise."

—◊◊◊—

The smell of autumn filled the air. Cora and I decided to take advantage of a bus trip to visit Salem, Massachusetts, where the fall colors were said to be spectacular. We also made plans to meet up with another internet Wiccan friend named Raven, who lived just outside Salem. Michael and the kids drove Cora and me to the bus stop, and soon we were on our way to a city known for its public Wiccan community. I had some reservations about going, since Michael was moody and often lashed out at the kids, but I made sure there was food in the house and money for them to do something fun, and hoped all would be well until my return.

It was evening when we arrived in Salem, so after checking into our hotel room and calling home to check in with my family, we met with Raven and headed into the historic seaside village.

It was déjà vu. We could definitely feel "energy" as we walked through town. All the shops were closed, so there was little activity in the streets except for one place: the Witches' Café, where we ate and talked about what places we wanted to visit.

We opted to join the morning bus tour, which included trips to The House of the Seven Gables and the Witch Museum, then we would head off on our own with Raven as our guide. Later we would meet up with the bus tour for dinner with a psychic since it was included in the trip. With our plans in place, we left the café, parted ways with Raven, and headed back to the hotel, excited about what tomorrow would bring.

After an early breakfast, our bus tour took us through the city, with a guide pointing out different points of interest. We found the Witch Museum itself was rather commercialized, but as I read the list of names of those who had been tried and killed for practicing witchcraft during the witch hysteria, one caught my eye—the name Sarah Wildes. We decided to ditch the bus tour to join Raven for a walk through the Old Burying Point Cemetery.

It was nice to be out of the broom closet, as we openly displayed our pentacles, flowing black capes, and witchy boots. Making a path through the rustling leaves, we came upon a large elderly tree with limbs that cast shadows on the graves below. I stood beneath it and Cora snapped a photo as a memory to mark the occasion. We then ventured into what seemed a labyrinth of faded tombstones until we found the stone monuments created for those who had been executed at the Salem witch trials.

Walking through the walled courtyard surrounded by empty stone benches that represented each victim who had been executed, we solemnly read their quotes imprinted on the ground. Suddenly, I glanced up to the bench cenotaph and read the familiar name, Sarah Wildes. I gasped and took a step backward but couldn't look away.

Out of nowhere, a short woman with auburn hair appeared. She looked at the stone, turned and looked me directly in my eyes, and said, "Sarah." Then she was gone.

Startled, I shrank back more because I now saw the name become my own. Cora and Raven were just as stunned as we looked around but couldn't find her. She had simply vanished.

"Ally, this has to do with reincarnation," Cora said.

Pausing to recall my bewildered senses, I reached for my pentacle around my neck and held it between my fingers. "I believe I was Sarah in a past life."

That night, we gathered in our hotel room and set up an altar with the tools we had either brought or had come across that day to create our own sacred space. After casting our magic circle and calling forth the four quarters, we invited the Lord and Lady into our circle of three. Outside, the wind howled and the full moon shone brightly upon the hundreds of others wherever they might be, entering that same sacred space.

—◠◠—

The night of my first Witches' Ball came. The costume affair was sponsored by Cerridwen's Cauldron, and I was dressed in attire to represent the goddess Epona. After adding a horse brooch to my cape as a finishing touch, I called to the kids from the bottom of the stairs to say goodbye.

Within seconds, the pitter-patter of little feet echoed down the wooded stairs in expectation of a hug. They stopped short as they looked at me bug-eyed. Their expression was priceless as I explained I was going to a Halloween party and that they would be dressing up and going trick-or-treating in a few days. Michael gave me a confounded look as he came from the kitchen, saying, "Who wants to make cookies?"

As I walked out the door, I asked the kids to save one for me.

Cora was waiting for me when I arrived at the ball. We decided to go inside and wait for a few more of our friends. As we neared the door, a meow greeted us. The spotted cat unknowingly set the feel for a Samhain night. (Samhain means summer's end; it's the witches' New Year and the feast of the dead, when those departed could return to the land of the living for this one night to celebrate with family and friends.)

Upon entering we noticed our names were at the top of the guest list. Since the tickets had stated they had the right to deny anyone entrance, I breathed a sigh of relief when we were handed a piece of parchment paper to write our desire for the new year. I wrote, *To be in a coven and further my psychic abilities.* We then stood in line to be smudged (when a feather is used to brush sage smoke over an individual to ward off negative energies). Amber and Conan, the owners of Cerridwen's Cauldron, seated us at the table next to their coven, and we saved seats for our friends who would be arriving shortly.

Before long, all the doors were locked since no one would be allowed to leave or enter once the Samhain ritual began. It was quite the sight to see, two hundred witches forming a circle around a huge painted pentagram on the center of the floor. Amber motioned us to the inner circle; there would be two more on the outside once everyone took their place. All the lights were shut off, making it pitch black except for the flicker of two candles on the altar casting light on the pumpkins, gourds, and fall foliage. The constant rhythm of tribal drumming was trance-inducing as Amber extended her staff above the crowd, walked around the perimeter, and recited words to cast the circle.

I could feel the power tingling through my body as energy was being raised. A coven member stood in the east and called forth the element of air while using an athame to draw a pentagram in the air, followed by three other coven members who called forth the elements of fire, water, and earth. As the incense was poured on the smoldering charcoal, the scent of patchouli, cinnamon, and dragon's blood filled the room. Salt water was sprinkled and the incense was carried, purifying the sacred space.

Amber slammed her staff down on the hardwood floor and, as if on cue, the drumming stopped. She then exclaimed, "The circle is now open."

Another coven member, who I would later learn was named Iris, stepped forward and spoke about the veil between the worlds being thinnest at this time of year. She explained this was a time to honor one's ancestors who had gone on before them.

Amber stood veiled before the altar as she invoked the Crone Goddess. The shadow of antlers appeared on the wall as Conan, who had taken his place in front of the altar, donned his antler crown and invoked the God. Then they faced one another, with her holding the chalice while he plunged his athame into the red wine, symbolically performing the Great Rite.

This was the time to silently honor a lost loved one, and I concentrated on my great-aunt. I had known she was the bishop in a spiritualist church but didn't know much else except family hearsay.

The silence was then broken as Amber offered words of thanks to the departed. We then made our way in procession outdoors, where a large cauldron was burning. While chanting, we each took our turn placing our parchment paper with our desire for the new year into the flames. The drum beat fast and wild as we danced around the flaming cauldron, hooting and hollering. With much merry-making, the circle was closed.

After the ritual, we returned inside for the feast. A full pig was displayed on the food table, complete with an apple in its mouth. Other foods and desserts surrounded it. The DJ took over, and everyone hit the dance floor. This was as elaborate as a wedding affair, except that everyone was in costume.

At the end of the night, Amber advised us that we would be

receiving an invitation to a private Samhain celebration with her coven to be held on the actual day of Samhain.

—〰—

I had just returned from picking up the newspaper, which included an article about the Witches' Ball, when the phone rang. Bo's voice was subdued as he explained that he and his wife had separated and divorce was imminent. She had met another man on the web and was moving to Iowa. Bo was upset by his wife's departure, which I could relate to because while Michael was with me physically, emotionally he was gone. Bo began calling me every day and soon we were eagerly anticipating our time together, though nothing inappropriate was ever said. That is, until the night before Thanksgiving.

That night, Bo whispered, "I feel there's this chemistry between you and me, one that I've never felt before. This connection between us is unique, and you seem to know my thoughts before I say them."

"I know what you mean." I could hardly restrain myself but managed to keep it together. "But I had associated it with a past life experience."

I already knew what he was going to say next. "You know I don't believe in past lives, but I do believe in soul mates. I think our relationship is even more than that. I believe this is all part of God's plan."

I had a hard time speaking due to the lump in my throat, but it didn't matter. In my mind, I was associating the term *soul mate* with the spell I thought hadn't worked. I remembered how I had blown off the idea that Bo could possibly be the one since he was married, but now all that had changed. Maybe we hadn't yet verbalized our feelings, but it was clear that our hearts had spoken.

A WITCH'S ENCOUNTER WITH GOD

CHAPTER NINE

—w—

Cora and I arrived at an open, rock-strewn area that resembled a blanket of boulders. We sat down on them, feeling the heat of the sun penetrating their smooth surface. On this rare warm Saturday in February, I confided in her about my long-distance relationship with Bo and his divorce plans.

"You know, I've never met him, but there's something about this guy that just doesn't set right," Cora said.

I stared at her. "Really? I feel as though I knew him in a past life and consider him my soul mate."

"That may be, but have you found out what kind of turmoil he brought into your past life?"

"I haven't considered that. I've felt as though we were perhaps lovers, which I believed was the reason for our strong connection."

Cora shook her head. "I don't like him. I don't have a good feeling about this, and besides, he's a born-again. All he wants is to win some brownie points for his God."

"You think so?" I knew all too well Christians' desire to convert everyone to their belief.

"He's probably thinking of you as a prize possession," she mused aloud, "one that would give him lots of favor with his God. With his narrow-minded way of thinking, he probably believes he's earning extra points by converting a witch."

"That'll never happen," I assured her. "Been there, done that, don't want to go back."

"There's just something about him," she warned. "Be careful of that thwart."

We walked the rocky path to the top of a waterfall, where we sat enjoying all the beauty the Mother Goddess had laid out before us. I spent time meditating, which brought a release from the stress I'd been feeling over the whole situation with Bo. I also decided it was time to try to work things out with Michael.

That night Michael and I really talked for the first time in a long time. We shared what had gone wrong in our marriage and where we were now. I brought up the topic of divorce, but Michael said he didn't have the finances to move out to his own apartment, which made it clear he had ruled out reconciliation. There was no heated argument, just a sharing of feelings that I had hoped for in our marriage but now seemed lost forever.

During the conversation, I realized that buried deep inside me I still had feelings for him. Had we really come to a place of irreconcilable differences? I cried myself to sleep, thinking of all I had hoped for and dreamt of versus what reality had become.

—⁓⁓—

Late on a Sunday morning a few weeks later, the kids stayed home with Michael while I drove to The Village to meet with Cora. We did some talking and shopping and ended up at Cerridwen's Cauldron.

It seemed as though Amber had been waiting for us. She said she had something important to discuss with us and invited us into the back room. There she talked about a woman's group she was organizing with several members from her coven, and she asked if we were interested. This was just what I had been waiting for—a group that met regularly and worked magic together. Cora and I immediately accepted, and we were told the first meeting would be at new moon and we should come prepared to do a spell of our choosing.

—m—

On the night of the new moon, the sky was starless as we made our way up to the temple room to work our spells. Amber opened the door, and we entered a shrine for the Goddess. A two-foot-tall statue of Isis and another of Osiris stood next to the altar. On the walls were plaques and paintings of many aspects of the Lady and her Lord, while the ceiling had a string of lights in the shape of a pentacle. We formed a circle around the altar, which was already set up.

Amber cast the circle, and other women in the coven called the quarters. After the sacred space was created, we agreed in unison, "So mote it be."

My turn came to cast the spell of my choice, and I timidly approached the altar with my suede pouch. I carefully arranged my mini cast iron cauldron on the altar top, and after anointing a green candle with oil, I placed it behind the cauldron that contained Epsom salt, rubbing alcohol, and herbs. After taking a deep breath, I began my chant.

Fear disappeared as I focused on my desired intent—a new vehicle. When I felt the energy peak, I took the parchment paper on which I had inscribed my desire and lit it with the candle before throwing it into the flaming cauldron. Once the flame went out, and with my spellwork complete, I returned to my place in the circle.

After the other women in the coven had completed their spells, the circle was closed. We then discussed how things had gone and scheduled upcoming meetings before going downstairs to the feast awaiting us.

—m—

Moonlight filtered softly through my bedroom window and illuminated my altar. I stood with Luna on my shoulder as I lit two silver taper candles, their flames dancing shadows against the wall. At each of the four quarters, tea lights glowed in appropriate-color holders. At the front center of the altar lay the pentacle. A clay dish of sea salt, a bowl of water, and an incense holder filled the remaining space.

I lit the incense, took a deep breath, and silently cast the magic circle. When magical space had been created, I sat in front of the altar. The door flew open, causing Luna to ruffle her feathers, as Michael barged in. He dropped his boots on the floor and removed the change from his pants pockets before climbing into bed, making sure to disrupt me. I thought his intrusion rather ignorant but determined that I wouldn't let it stop my full moon ritual.

Ignoring him, I began to mediate, and after what seemed like only a few moments, I realized that one-third of the candles had already melted. Part of the wax dripped from the Goddess candle, falling in an unusual fashion and ending up clear across the table in the bowl of water. When I looked into the water bowl, there was a complete wax image of a serpent wrapped around the body of a motherly figure.

I stood amazed at how the wax had managed to get from the candle into the water bowl. Then I stared at the image itself, which was unlike any other Goddess image I had seen before. I quickly took down the circle, removed the wax image from the water, and put it away for safekeeping. To my relief but not my surprise, Michael had slept through the whole thing.

I knew without a shadow of a doubt I had just experienced something significant in the magical realm. I waited in eager anticipation for the next leg of this amazing journey.

CHAPTER TEN

—m—

T he full moon rose high in the dark night sky as we gathered at Cerridwen's Cauldron for ritual. I was glad to be part of a coven and working energy within a group, as I believed it would aid in my growth and magical abilities. After the ritual debrief, Amber told us she had a task for each of us to complete before the next full moon.

We were to create something using the specific material she would assign to each of us. I was told to create something made of clay, and immediately the figure of the Goddess that had mysteriously materialized in the water bowl on my altar came to mind. I could already feel it stirring inside me and couldn't wait to get started. Somehow the fact that I knew nothing of sculpting or even how to draw an image didn't seem problematic. I wrote down the task I was given along with what I was going to make.

The next day between bus runs, I stopped at the local arts and crafts store to purchase the clay and plastic sculpting tools for my project. Then in the quiet of my empty house, I spread newspapers to protect the dining room table, placed the clay and tools down, and lit a candle and some incense. Before long, I was in a trance state, placing my hands on the block of clay.

When completed, the work of art I'd created amazed me. It matched exactly the figure of the wax Goddess that had mysteriously transferred from the candle to the water bowl that night on my altar. I had absolutely no experience with clay, yet my piece was complete and seemed to have just come into being.

When the next cycle of the full moon approached, we gathered again for ritual. This time, each of the coven members brought what they had handcrafted out of the material they had been told to use. What each of us had conjured up was amazing. I peeled back the velvet cover of my piece, revealing her raw beauty.

Amber gasped as her eyes lit up her entire face. "Wow, she's amazing! Put her on the altar." As I placed her next to the goddess candle, she asked, "Do you know her name?"

"When I asked, all that was said to me was, I am She,'" I said.

"Then you must find out. You already know who She is, but search until you are sure."

Over the next few months, I expanded my studies in search of the goddess image that I had created. I finally stumbled upon an article describing the exact description of my goddess figurine. It had been unearthed at an oracle in Delphi. No reproduction of this image had ever been made, yet thousands of years later I had created an exact replica without ever having seen it or knowing of it—not in this life anyway. I began to work with Mother Energy in my own magical space.

On Mother's Day, the kids and I picked up my mom to go out for brunch at a diner my mom was fond of. We caught up while eating, and Mom was pleased to hear that I was no longer attending New Zion, as she considered them a cult. She did acknowledge that the church had a hands-on approach in helping my family when we were in need, but went on to say that she would've preferred if I continued in the family tradition and returned to the Episcopal church she and Dad attended.

Although I was practicing prediction, I couldn't foretell her reaction when I told her I was a witch.

"What next? Wait until your father hears this one!" Mom said with a grin. "You know, your great-aunt was a bishop at one of those spiritualist churches, but I don't believe in any of that stuff."

That evening, I felt compelled to call the woman I had always considered my "spiritual mom." We hadn't spoken in a long time, and all I wanted was to wish Joan a happy Mother's Day despite our spiritual differences.

"Happy Mother's Day!" I said when she answered the phone.

"Why, thank you," Joan responded. "I hope you enjoyed your day as well."

I went on to share about taking my mom out for brunch that morning and how Michael and the kids were doing, but the conversation couldn't stop there.

"I wish you could've heard the teaching John gave today about God's role for mothers and the impact they have on their children," she said.

I really didn't care about the word John preached that or any day, but her words jabbed my emotions to respond. "I couldn't have heard it if I wanted. I'm not allowed!"

Before I knew it, I was in the middle of another debate over God, the devil, and my life. We simply couldn't have a normal conversation any longer. I always ended up defending witchcraft while Joan condemned it. All too quickly, I reminded her that the reason I called was to wish her a happy Mother's Day, not to get into a debate.

Joan said, "Thank you," then dismissed herself since she had other things to do.

Tired and sweaty, we drove home from the park in a hot car with no air conditioning. With the windows wide open, it felt like we were standing in front of hair dryers. Michael was driving, and just as we approached the exit off-ramp that eventually merged into the road we were on, a car driven by a thirty-something man accelerated and attempted to cut us off.

To my surprise, Michael sped up, challenging to get in front of the car as he yelled four-letter words. The other driver replied in kind, and the kids and I became unwilling participants in a street race as the two men drove side by side, each one swerving back and forth to avoid contact while trying to force the other off the road. The cars were so close that I could've easily reached out and touched the other driver. Terror froze all the kids' expressions.

"Michael, it's not worth it," I pleaded, "Let him go ahead for the kids' sake."

He accelerated again, and the other car followed suit as the two lanes became one, causing Michael to swerve into the oncoming lane. Driving head-on toward us was a woman who looked horrified. There was no room to pull over on the narrow two-lane bridge she was crossing, and soon we were playing a deadly game of chicken with our lives in the balance.

"Michael, stop!" I screamed.

He put the pedal to the metal and pulled in front of his opponent, cutting him off and just missing the oncoming car.

I could hardly breathe as we pulled up to the red light. The other driver was now banging on Michael's window, calling him out.

"Let it go!" I pleaded.

The light turned green and Michael sped away, and thankfully the car didn't follow.

My heart still pounded as we pulled into our driveway. "You could've killed us!"

He didn't say a thing; he just got out of the car and walked into the house like nothing had happened. The other maniac's wild hair, glasses, and look that could kill would be imprinted on my memory forever.

That was the last time we rode with Michael.

—⟶⟨∙⟩⟵—

The last day of school was a half day, so I expected to finish up early. I ended up with only a handful of kids on the bus, and after making only three stops, I headed back to the bus yard. After quickly sweeping the bus floor and gathering the books I had hidden under my seat, I headed for the car, glad to be done early so I could stop home and find a better hiding place for them before I had to pick up my own kids. The tension between Michael and me regarding witchcraft had eased, but I didn't want to leave the books in open view.

Within fifteen minutes, I was pulling into my driveway. Cujo greeted me at the door, wagging his tail at my return home. I bounded upstairs and made some space at the bottom of the old cedar chest that held out-of-season clothing, then placed my books there. Michael would never go into it, so I figured they would be safe yet easily accessible. After all was secure, I left to go get the kids.

Summer was officially here, with the temperature hitting the nineties as early as ten a.m. Without air conditioning, our home quickly became unbearable, so the kids went out to the tree-shaded yard while I finished cleaning the house. I had just decided that would be all I could accomplish in this heat when the phone rang.

"Hi, what are you up to?" Amber asked.

"Nothing really. Just finished up with the housework, but it's so hot, I'm already beat."

"Well, the reason I'm calling is because I know you're off for the summer and I'm home now during the week because I have my kids home from school. I'm going to be making incense and oils. I was thinking maybe you could come over and give me a hand. You can bring your kids. Maybe they can help keep mine busy so I can get some work done. At least you can get out of that oven and into someplace cool."

"Sure, sounds good to me," I answered. "We can be there in about forty minutes if that's okay."

"That'll work. See you when you get here."

I hung up the phone and called the kids inside. When we arrived at Amber's, they quickly disappeared into her children's bedrooms while Amber and I went down to the basement, where a table and chairs were set up with an enormous amount of different herbs. I knew how to grind the herbs to powder form but had never blended them specifically for spells and rituals. Since I hadn't worked much with oils, such as blending them to create a specific desired intent to be used in circle or invoking a specific goddess, doing so would be a great learning experience.

We spent hours working in the basement, completing an ample supply of some of the fastest-selling incense and oils, though we barely made a dent in the list of items needed in the shop. Summer was always the busiest time of year, mostly due to their location. Then the kids started to get antsy, coming down every few minutes to see if we were finished yet.

We were surprised to see it was almost dinnertime, so when Amber asked us to stay and ordered pizza, the kids were delighted. We spent the next few hours talking and relaxing, and Amber asked if we could come back again tomorrow. I readily agreed, looking forward to another day with her.

Later that night, Amber called and asked me to do a reading in a divination method of my choice and let her know the outcome the next day. I decided to use the stone runes I had made and infused with my own energy.

After Michael and the kids were fast asleep, I quietly opened the cedar chest in my bedroom and took out the pouch that held my runes. I made my way down to the living room and laid a special cloth that I used for readings on the marble coffee table. Once a candle and some incense were lit, I held the runes in my hand while meditating on Amber's business.

When I was about to put them back in the pouch to mix them and cast them, I heard someone on the stairs. I gripped the pouch beneath my shirt, only to see the green glowing eyes of Gypsy, my cat. She jumped onto the couch and curled up in my lap, adding her energy to my reading. After picking the stones and laying them in place, I turned them over one by one and interpreted the meaning of each stone. A major conflict that would have a negative impact on the business became clear, but at least the outcome seemed to be in Amber's favor.

I was troubled by the findings, so the kids and I left for Amber's earlier than we did yesterday. The children ran off to play a game of hide and seek, and as Amber and I went down to the basement, she asked the result of my reading. I showed her the two runes that were picked and gave my interpretation, and she confirmed that was what others had found as well.

While we worked on making incense and oils, she explained some conflicting business issues she was having. We discussed the situation, and she asked me to do another reading that night to ask what her next move should be. (Those changes came into play at the shop not long after my readings.)

Over the next few weeks, I continued making the incense and oils with Amber and really got to know her on a more personal level. She became not only my high priestess but also my friend. We would spend the day together and often talked on the phone at night. I was so preoccupied with working magic, helping Amber, and doing other coven-related things that I didn't think much about the loss of my former church family.

As summer came to an end, Cora and I went on an excursion to my favorite beach, an oasis with rolling sand dunes and tidal marshes. The cries of seagulls could be heard far out over the endless sea, and the pristine shoreline stretched for miles. It was a natural habitat away from the sound of boardwalks and amusements, and I thought Cora would really appreciate the song of the roaring blue-green ocean.

We found a secluded strip of beach where the nearest people were half a mile away. Preparing for ritual, we smoothed the sand and laid down our celestial blanket. She and I had already gathered a few seashells, and we placed one filled with sand in the north, one holding our incense in the east, a burning candle jar in the south; and a shell filled with ocean water in the west. All the elements being accounted for, we dug a hole in the sand, attempting to build a fire pit.

The pit was filled with twigs and driftwood, then we attempted to ignite it to no avail. The fire was no match for the wind that day. We chuckled at ourselves as Cora said, "Here we are, two witches unable to invoke fire in our circle!" We laughed even harder.

After we gained our composure, it was time to focus on creating our magical space. I pressed *play* on our music player, and the musical chant "We All Come from the Goddess" set the tone for our ritual. Using a long branch, I cast the magic circle in the sand. We took turns calling the quarters before focusing on healing energy for the ocean. Then when our magical work was done, we released the circle, emptied the shell with the sand, and took the shell of water back to the ocean.

There, I pulled up my broomstick skirt and tied it, allowing myself freedom to splash in the surf. Cora joined me, and I turned just in time to meet a breaker by surprise. As the ebb and flow of the tide created an undertow covering our feet in sand, I looked out and saw what looked like a dolphin in the surf. "Look, a dolphin!" I pointed it out for Cora to see, but the dolphin was no longer there.

Out of the swelling sea, on the crest of a wave, a mound of seafoam emerged. We watched in amazement as the foam transformed into the shape of a beautiful woman right before our eyes. Born of the ocean and formed by the wind was Aphrodite, Goddess of the Sea. Foam flowers were strewn throughout her hair, and she skimmed over the water effortlessly before disappearing under the crashing waves and being drawn back into the deep.

CHAPTER ELEVEN

—〰—

B y the time Michael got home from work, I was already twenty-five minutes late for our first pagan festival in the mountains. My late arrival frustrated Amber, as we soon found ourselves sitting in rush-hour traffic. I called home to check on the children. While I was concerned about leaving them home with their father for the weekend, I'd put a lot of planning into a peaceful atmosphere in the house before I left.

I was outraged to learn that, while I was en route to Amber's, she had called my house looking for me and told my daughter she wasn't waiting any longer and to expect me home soon. My daughter Lynn had been sitting on our porch steps since that call, waiting for my return. As I tried to comfort and reassure her over the phone, I was half tempted to get out of the car and walk home.

We soon broke out of the heavy traffic, and I calmed down as we drove. About five hours later, we reached the long, winding dirt road that led to the woods where Lady Brandilyn, the mother coven's high priestess, and her coven had been camping. We were directed through a makeshift parking area to a small registration booth. After signing in, we drove down the road, passing a stage where a pagan band played.

We were surrounded by hundreds of acres of desolate land below a pitch-black sky where lanterns provided the only light. Lady Brandilyn pointed us to a clearing where we were to set up our tent, and after Amber and I were settled and had a quick bite to eat, Lady Brandilyn told us the fire circle would begin shortly at the mountaintop meeting site. "You ladies get laid and have a great time!" she called as Amber and I started toward it.

Amber and I looked at each other, then burst out laughing like teenagers who were surprised to hear such a thing from their mother's mouth. As we walked up the mountainside, low rhythmic drumming carried through the trees. Huge flames reached skyward when we reached the fire circle in the clearing at the top of the mountain. We worked our way through the outer circle, where caped witches shielded themselves against the cool midnight wind.

Closer to the fire, drummers sat in one section of the circle while skyclad (naked) witches danced to the beat of the primal drum, keeping in rhythm with one another. The pulsating of the drums vibrated the earth where we stood. Beneath the glowing full moon, in the warmth of the fire and among others of a like mind, was exactly where I'd always wanted to be.

Then a thought occurred to me: Could the glowing flames and intense heat be preparation for the afterlife that I had been taught awaited those who chose not to follow Christ? Then I wondered if it even mattered anyway. Dancing to the beat of the drum seemed a pretty cool way to spend eternity. I shrugged off the thought as three merry and gregarious women approached us with a basket full of condoms they were selling. Lady Brandilyn's words came to mind as Amber and I looked at each other and chuckled.

We didn't leave the fire circle and make our way back to camp until just before dawn, so it was near noon when we awoke. Rushing water sounded in the distance, and after a cup of coffee, Amber and I took a walk to explore the area. Arriving in the dark of the night, we hadn't been able to see the beauty of the mountains reaching high above a free-flowing river complete with a waterfall. The land we walked was beautiful with all the elements—earth, air, fire, and water—all flowing together in perfect harmony.

Our afternoon was filled with attending seminars and browsing the handcrafted tools, clothing, and jewelry sold by vendors. That evening, pagan music again filled the air and the fire dance generated its own energy around the fire circle. A world that existed outside the everyday lives we lived was a place filled with magic and energy—a world between worlds, a sacred space.

As I soon learned, the intense energy of magical space tends to reveal whatever issues one needs to work out in their life. The coven was already experiencing some friction regarding mundane responsibilities. After a few hours of listening to their debate, Amber and I slipped away to the fire circle, where we connected with some people we knew from back home.

After the spiral dance, the next pagan band took the stage. Their first song was a mockery of Christianity, which annoyed me. We often spoke of how Christians condemned us, and yet here we were doing the same. In that instant I remembered Pastor John's words to me: "The day will come when they'll turn you against anything to do with Christ." At the time, I'd told him that he couldn't be further from the truth. Now I bore witness to the hypocrisy.

The next morning, I awoke before Amber and let her sleep. I quietly exited our tent and headed for the makeshift kitchen for a cup of coffee. Most of the coven was up, and they all seemed more relaxed than the previous night. Lady Brandilyn was exceptionally warm and invited me to sit and talk with her while we waited for Amber to awaken. We would be leaving today, and though I looked forward to returning home to my children, a part of me wanted to remain there on the mountainside where the wind whispered through the leaves in the forest, the song of the river never ended, and magic was afoot. My weekend experience had definitely been worth the minor conflict Amber and I experienced at the start of the trip.

—◠◠—

Our drive home was long and tiring, as our lack of sleep had finally caught up with us. When we stopped for dinner on the way, we realized that the adjustment back to the reality of everyday life would take some time. Energy still flowed through me as it had while I was in sacred space, but with it came the recognition that the festival had made clear some things that I needed to deal with. Amber and I had put aside our differences, but I couldn't resolve the song mocking Christians.

A few days after I returned home, I called Pastor John. I'm not sure if I was missing the fatherly bond I once had or my misplaced allegiance to him, but just hearing his voice heartened me. My call surprised him, but he was pleased to hear that all was well with the children.

"Is there a particular reason for your call?" he then asked. "Have you come to your senses and decided to come back to Jesus?"

"No. Sorry to disappoint you." I hesitated. "But there is something that I wanted to talk to you about. I ... just came home from a pagan festival."

After a few seconds of silence, he asked sarcastically, "So how was it dancing around in your birthday suit underneath the moon?"

"The term is *skyclad.*" Perturbed, I went on, "But that's not what I called about. One of the songs at the festival disturbed me because it was mocking Christianity."

"Well, hallelujah! I'm happy to hear you at least have some kind of discernment left, and saw that something about this new lifestyle of yours isn't good. I haven't heard that from you in a long time."

His response confused me. "Well, it's not discernment. It's just that I'm one for being fair regardless of the belief system."

"Did you really think they would act fairly when it comes to Christians and things of God?" he asked. "Oh, that's right. You think your white magic or whatever you want to call it is good."

"I know that's hard for you to understand, and I really don't want to get in a debate over magic being black or white."

"Okay. Then why don't you come see what God is doing instead of dancing around in your birthday suit with a bunch of people who make fun of God?"

Our conversation pretty much ended at that point with Pastor John stuck on the skyclad issue. Even so, I was happy to have talked with him and in some strange way felt better having voiced my discomfort with the mockery. I'd missed speaking with him and respected his opinion even though we disagreed. If only he could accept me for who I was and not just who he thought I should be.

Why was it that, even after being abandoned by God, I still had a perilous loyalty to Pastor John?

A WITCH'S ENCOUNTER WITH GOD

CHAPTER TWELVE

—⚬—

T he time came for me to leave for the coven meeting at Amber's house. I finished the last row of stitching on my robe for this year's Samhain Ball and quickly slipped it on, contemplating what I would look like after my face was painted and my hair dyed. It fit perfectly! After hanging my newly crafted robe on the back of my bedroom door, I grabbed my purse, kissed the children goodbye, and headed for the ball-planning meeting.

I found it hard to believe that an entire year had passed since my first Witches' Ball. I was now part of a coven, which was exactly what I had written on the parchment paper as my desire last year. This ball would be different though, as I was now actively planning it with the coven and had no idea how much preparation went into such a big event. After we worked out all the mundane details, the ritual itself became the topic of discussion.

Amber started announcing the coveners who would be calling quarters, and I looked up from my notepad as she called out my name. "You're calling west."

Wow. This was the first time I was asked to call a quarter.

"Don't worry. You'll do just fine," she added as if reading my thoughts. "I wouldn't ask you unless I knew you were ready."

"That's cool. I'm comfortable with that." I felt both honored and panicked at the thought of how many people would be attending and the media surrounding the event.

—⚬—

The kids and I returned home after trick-or-treating. Missy still had her witch's hat on as she ran to Michael to show him the candy she'd collected. Lynn then removed her hooded robe and took her candy to him for inspection. Aaron swung his fake knife around as if part of his costume was in a fight with unseen forces. My face was already painted as a flaming mask, but I needed to get into the rest of my costume attire, so I ran upstairs to the bedroom.

Once robed and ready to go, I said goodbye to the kids and headed for the same location the ball had been held at the year prior. Cora was inside helping with the finishing touches of decorating the hall, and after smudging, I carried in the tray of cupcakes I'd made. I placed them on the dessert table, then put my shawl on the back of my seat at the coven table and went to join the others in final preparations.

Soon the place was packed. Last call was made for anyone who wanted to leave before the doors were locked, the lights went out, and the drumming began. I took my place in the west as Amber cast the magic circle before motioning for east to be called, followed by south. Then it was my turn. I faced west and held both arms high with my athame in one hand, took a deep breath, and focused on the water element. Calling forth the Guardians of the West, I drew the invoking pentagram in the air and concluded, "Hail and welcome."

A hundred and fifty pagans said the same.

The rest of the ball flew by as I kept busy helping behind the scenes. Afterward, Cora and I joined Amber and the rest of the coven in taking down decorations and cleaning up.

Not a soul was on the road as I drove home. Once there, I turned off the Halloween lights on our porch and, exhausted, collapsed in bed next to a comatose Michael.

—m—

The morning after the ball, I opened the newspaper and there

I was on the second page. After reading the well-written article, I emailed Bo to tell him about my public appearance: *Did you have fun at your friend's last night? Hope so, for your own well-being. Hey ... get this! My picture is in the newspaper today from the ball last night. I can send you a copy of the paper later on today. Write and let me know how you're doing.*

He quickly replied, *What's this, you're becoming a public witch now? Is it a good thing for people to see you and associate you with being a witch? I don't know if that's something you should let out to everyone. I mean with me, it's okay because I don't have a problem with it, but others may not think as I do. I'm doing alright, I went to a friend's and handed out candy to all the little ghosts and goblins, even witches!*

I answered, *So ... you think you were handing out candy to little witches, hey ... well, you would have been in for a real treat had you come last night! And you ... what's this about it not being a good idea in going public? It's what I believe in, and you wouldn't think twice about being in an article about Christmas, would you?*

My relationship with Bo continued comfortably until I learned he was going to be in the area visiting his family for Thanksgiving. The thought of spending time with Bo delighted me, but I also felt somewhat apprehensive about being alone with him. Cora had called him a vulture ready to entrap me in an attempt to win his Christian brownie points. I was unsettled about his intentions, so I carefully planned to have friends around to avoid temptation and prevent our relationship from going beyond an acceptable level of friendship.

Before I picked the kids up for Thanksgiving break, I cast a protection spell to suppress any lustful desires between Bo and me. Michael was getting out of the tub when the kids and I got home, and he dressed for dinner. We had just sat down to eat when we were interrupted by a knock at the door

The police, along with several others I had never seen before, stood on the porch looking for Michael. After talking outside with them for about fifteen minutes, he came back in, put on his shoes, and mumbled something about going with them to the hospital.

I was shocked. "The hospital? Are you sick?"

"Things are all messed up," he muttered as he searched for his other shoe. "The finances are so bad we'll probably lose the house, and I can't take it anymore."

Taking advantage of the delay, I went outside to talk with the police and crisis counselors. It turned out that Michael had been speaking to people at work about being depressed, and had been in contact with crisis counselors at the hospital just before I'd returned home with the children. Apparently, what he said caused them such concern that they came to the house to evaluate him. None of it made any sense to me. I just thought Michael was being his usual uncommunicative self.

"What was Michael doing when you got home this evening?" the woman from the crisis center asked.

"He was getting out of the bathtub."

"Has he seemed depressed?" the other counselor, a tall, hefty man, questioned.

"He never mentioned anything about it," I told them, still confused by what was going on.

"Did you know he called us earlier today?"

I shook my head. "No. I started making dinner as soon as I got home with the children. As a matter of fact, we were just sitting down to eat."

"We were here a few weeks ago when an internet friend of his called, concerned for his well-being," a police officer interjected.

"I remember that night." I thought back a few weeks. "But he said you were here concerning the car inspection sticker. I thought that rather odd at eleven o'clock at night, but then you left so I forgot all about it."

"Michael assured us that he was okay and had family here to support him," the officer said.

"He never mentioned anything about it to me, but then again, he rarely mentions anything anymore."

"One more thing," the crisis counselor said. "Michael said something about you being a witch. We were wondering if he's delusional."

Even as she asked the question, my mind was racing. If I denied being a witch, then they would surely think Michael was insane, but if I said I was, what would the repercussions be? Wicca was a recognized religion, but I needed to answer her question in the correct way. "Michael is not too fond of the fact that I'm involved with a nature-based religion called Wicca. That's probably why he mentioned it."

"I've heard of Wicca," she responded. "Thank you for the information. Now we know he's not delusional, because that would lead us to other concerns. We'll take it from here."

With that, Michael came out of the house and climbed into the back of the squad car, and they drove him away.

Now, how would I explain to the kids that the police and these strangers just took their dad away when I didn't understand any of it myself? And had my admission to practicing Wicca presented a problem? I packed up all my magical possessions just in case and called Amber. She gave me the number for a witches' defense lawyer in case I ran into any trouble, and confirmed my belief that we had the same constitutional rights as any other religion, though sometimes that was put to the test.

As I put my children to bed, I explained the best I could about Michael being sick and going to the hospital. Thankfully, they just accepted what I said and asked for their customary bedtime story. Then I waited for hours until I finally got a call from Michael saying he was being admitted. I climbed into my empty bed, trying to understand the secrets he kept and the lies he'd told me. What was the truth, and why was he so afraid to share it?

Then it hit me. Just how bad was our mortgage situation?

—⟋⟍⟍⟍—

The following evening, I drove my kids to their grandparents' house, reminded them to finish their homework, and headed for the hospital to visit Michael. I took the elevator to the eighth floor, only to be met by a locked door when I got off. After ringing the buzzer, I announced my name and who I'd come to see through the intercom. The door opened and I walked down the hall to a common recreation room that was occupied by mentally disturbed people, none of whom were Michael. I felt uneasy and vulnerable, even afraid, as I found a nurse and asked for Michael.

She went to get him, returning a few seconds later with him by her side. We took a seat on one of the several sofas, but I felt awkward and didn't know what to say. Michael didn't discuss what had happened, only asking, "Can you bring me some change so I can call home?"

I said I would, knowing my questions would remain unanswered. Oddly enough, Michael took me on a tour of the rec room as if we were at a house-warming party. Within a half hour, he stated, "You should get going since the kids need to get to bed."

I anxiously took him up on the suggestion and hurried to find someone to unlock the door so I could get out. At the elevator, I pushed the button and waited for what seemed an eternity for the elevator to reach the eighth floor. Once inside, I let out a sigh of relief.

I picked up the kids, who had already eaten dinner with their grandparents, so when we got home, I sent them upstairs to get ready for bed. With my clothes ready for the next day, I made sure the kids had everything they needed and then tucked them in.

That's when I received a call from Bo. He was in town, not far from where I lived, and on hearing my voice, he knew something was wrong. I told him about the latest turn of events and how upsetting it was. He drove to my home, and over the next few days, he spent time with us and offered me emotional support as I tried to sort through the broken pieces of my life. So much for the plans I had so carefully prepared so I wouldn't be alone with Bo. Fate sure had a will of its own.

Michael was diagnosed with manic depression, or bipolar disorder, a mental illness characterized by major mood swings. The social worker at the hospital described it as a chemical imbalance in the brain, and told me that with medication and therapy, Michael could return to being the man I married. This explained his major mood swings and volatile behavior, and gave me hope that our marriage could be salvaged.

I called the mortgage company to find out how bad it was. When they referred me to an attorney, that alone spoke volumes. How could Michael have let it get this bad? Six months ago, my mom had washed her hands of the mortgage responsibility after Michael refused to pay up. I remember her look of frustration as she handed him the mortgage book along with a strong warning not to ask for help again.

We certainly couldn't ask the church for money, so I was against the wall. After I explained the situation to the attorney, he made me a generous offer: I would avoid any fees if I paid the past-due balance. That was good news, except where would I come up with six months' worth of mortgage payments?

Bo stopped by the house on his way to the airport. When he asked what had me so upset and I told him the news, he was speechless. Then he wrote me a check for the past-due balance.

—m—

Michael returned home, but he was far from the person he had once been. Not only did he refuse to talk about his issues, but he quickly took up permanent residency in bed. I got the kids to school and went to work, but Michael made no attempt to get up. His employer was sympathetic regarding his illness, though I was quickly losing patience.

The entire house was now walking on eggshells, not knowing when Michael would have another episode.

The noise from the kids playing was enough to set him off. Out of nowhere one day, I heard Michael's roar and the thud of a book being thrown against the wall. As I went upstairs to see what was wrong, Michael screamed, "Shut up, you stupid moron!"

I walked into the bedroom and almost fell victim to the next airborne book. "What's wrong?" I asked.

He mumbled something about noise before climbing back in bed, turning over, and going back to sleep. When I checked on the kids, they were silent and panic stricken. I calmed them down, then closed their bedroom door to contain any noise and called his therapist.

She explained that Michael had decided he wanted to keep his counseling sessions confidential and there was no immediate plan for the rest of the family to be included. When I attempted to explain my concerns about Michael's behavior, she insisted that Michael was adamant that she not discuss his condition with me.

I gave up. What else could I do? My hope that this new diagnosis would be the catalyst of a renewed marriage was gone.

CHAPTER THIRTEEN

—ɯɯ—

I kept my cell phone turned on in case chaos broke out at home with Michael and the kids. After a stressful week, I was glad to be going to The Village to meet up with Amber and unwind. We ate lunch, then returned to the shop and retreated to the back room, where Amber had a candle burning in a glass jar. As I gazed into the flame, images began to emerge.

"Interesting, isn't it?" Amber said as she sat next to me.

"I see a complete image of the Horned God here on this side." I carefully turned the jar to see what other images had taken form on the glass. A large tree formed from the wax, with its branches spreading out in amazing detail on the sides of the jar. "Wow, take a look at this!" I handed the jar to Amber.

She turned it to examine the intricate image. "There's something —or rather, someone—in your life that is a cause of heartache and a source of destruction that has to go."

I realized she was talking about Michael. She was right about him bringing sorrow into my life, but he had stopped going to church and was far from what you would call a Christian.

"You are a priestess, and Goddess would have a magical man in your life," she continued.

The thought of a magical man was enticing. I had always wanted a partner to work magic with and someone to accompany me to circles. "I believe Michael can stay as long as he doesn't stand in the way of my magical growth."

She eyed me. "And you don't see him as standing in the way?"

"There was a time, but not anymore." Michael didn't hold on to much of anything now.

"He still holds his Christian beliefs, does he not?"

"I suppose so, but his Christianity is never a topic of discussion."

"There is one who is better for you that Goddess is waiting to send, and it's not that born-again either." She stood, turned the jar slightly, and held it right in front of my eyes. "What do you see here?"

"A birthing," I replied after carefully looking at it. "I see a woman giving birth."

"New beginnings." Amber nodded as she set the jar down.

My cell phone rang, and I answered to hear the frantic cries of my daughter yelling that Michael was on another rampage. He ranted loudly in the background. I told Amber I had to go and hurried out the door.

My heart raced almost as quickly as my car the entire ride home. There, I ran into the house, only to find the girls locked in their room and Michael fast asleep.

I stared at two chalices set before me. Which would I choose? They looked pretty much the same, so I picked up one of the herbal brews and placed it to my lips. A distinct aroma that I couldn't place went up my nostrils as I drank down the bitter concoction.

Our high priest, dressed in Shamanic garb, took my hand and gently pulled me to my feet. He handed me my celestial blanket and led me out into the night, where I could feel the vibrations of the earth beneath my bare feet as he guided me on the mountainside trail. I unfurled my blanket and sat down in the place he chose, then watched as he cast a circle of protection around me.

When finished, he left me alone in the still of the night.

I looked into a starless sky on this dark moon night and shivered in the cold air. It seemed like I sat for hours, listening to the song of crickets and the wind rustling through the leaves, though I had no concept of time until I realized I wasn't alone. I blinked and did a double take at seeing silver-white lights creating their own magical spiral. They encircled me, and a few disappeared into the trees only to return a few seconds later. I watched entranced by the fairy realm until they vanished as quickly as they appeared.

Someone approached from behind, and I turned to find my high priest reaching for my hand again. I got up, grabbed my blanket, and followed him back down the trail. After I was bound and blindfolded, he led me to the gateway of magical space where I met the God of Death. I felt the cold blade at my throat, and for a brief second fear ran through me as I was told to state my name. He asked a few questions that I must have answered right because I was granted entrance.

I faced my own symbolic death buried beneath a black shroud, then I was brought before the Devouress of the Dead. Standing before her, I gave my declaration of innocence and pledged my commitment to the Goddess, crossing the threshold into the afterlife. I gazed into the mirror and saw my reflection of the Goddess within, wearing her crown. Amber placed her hands on me and transferred power that can best be described as a vibrating energy that surged through my entire body. I was given my Craft name and welcomed into the coven. With the ceremony now complete, it was time to celebrate.

"Stop! Don't go in there!" The man stood on the pavement outside the witch shop, confronting potential customers like a door-to-door salesman. He held a Bible in his hand, and several others joined him in parading around the perimeter of the shop, leaving a trail of tracts. The born-agains were back!

I stepped outside and sat on the front steps as he proclaimed, "Don't go in there! It's the devil's workshop!"

The shoppers walked on by, most ignoring his urgent pleas to avoid evil and a few accepting tracts just to be polite. "You're in danger of burning in eternal damnation!" He pointed to Cerridwen's Cauldron.

Anger rose within me. If he and his companions wanted to tell of their love for Jesus, so be it, but why condemn another belief? Most of the people seemed annoyed at their presence or laughed at their accusations. Anyone who wanted to come in the shop simply walked around them and entered anyway.

They grew louder and more annoying, so I asked the fire-breathing evangelist, "Do you really feel you're representing a loving God here with your actions?"

He turned from handing out tracts and looked surprised to find a woman dressed in witchy clothes addressing him "God is a God of love, but He also despises sin."

"Right, and didn't He send His Son because of sin?"

"He sent Jesus for forgiveness," he said, giving me his full attention.

"So tell me, am I right in saying that Jesus Himself said that He came into this world *not* to condemn it?"

The man seemed a bit unsettled about where this conversation was going, but determined to gain the upper hand, he answered, "He did, but He also said He came to save the lost and dying world. That's what we're here for, to tell about the salvation of the Lord."

"So exactly how do you intend to tell people about salvation while you stand here and condemn them?"

"God is against evil." He looked at me more closely. "You seem to know quite a bit about Jesus. Perhaps you've been searching. His love is there for you too, you know?"

I smiled. "I knew Jesus. I used to follow Him. I was a born-again just like you."

He stared. "What happened?"

"Well, let's just say I decided to follow the Goddess."

His whole countenance changed. "You were born again, but now you've become a witch? You're doomed to hellfire for all eternity."

"Oh, now you're preaching hellfire for all eternity?" I snapped. "What happened to salvation?"

"You can't be saved, having known the Lord and reverted to the devil." He threw his hands in the air. "There's no use. You're doomed for eternity to the pit of fire!"

I stood my ground. "This doesn't seem very loving. Who do you think you are to condemn me?"

Another voice interrupted our conversation. "Go away and leave them alone. Take your religious rhetoric elsewhere. You don't see these people picketing your churches! Go away. No one wants you here."

The shop owner next door wasn't a witch, but he was obviously tired of listening to this man preach and bother potential customers.

The born-again man ignored the shopkeeper, still focused on me. "Your soul is lost and you'll spend forever in the lake of fire."

"When did you become God and decide my fate?" I asked. "Who are you to judge me?"

Amber stepped outside and called me away from him. "Don't waste your time. The police are on their way," she said as we walked back inside. "Born-agains! They have nothing better to do than leave tracts in my books and try to ruin business. Do they ever stop to think that this is someone's livelihood?"

I stood by the open door as the people in the shop spoke of the judgmental Christian God who was foreign to the ways of man and had little or no concern for mankind. Outside, the born-agains continued trying to keep the passersby from entering what they called a place of evil.

"Don't go in there," they pleaded. "Jesus would have you avoid evil at all cost."

As I stood between these two conflicting groups, I thought, *Jesus wouldn't have stood on the sidewalk handing out tracts. He would have walked right in and invited all of us to come have dinner with Him at the café across the street.* I thought back to my Christian days when my own determination to save souls inspired me to hand out tracts at the local mall. Now, with the shoe on the other foot, I realized all it really did was annoy people and push them away from God rather than draw them to Him.

A police car pulled up, and two officers walked toward the born-agains. I couldn't hear what was said, but a few moments later the police told us the born-agains would relocate elsewhere. I knew from experience that even though they would no longer be right outside our door, at some church somewhere nearby there'd be a whole lot of spiritual warfare going on.

CHAPTER FOURTEEN

—◊—

The gathering of robed witches drumming and dancing in the moonlight didn't seem to bother the neighbors, but the circle had barely closed when Amber called it a night, declaring it time to go feast. Initially bewildered by her rush to get the ritual over and done with, I then realized she was making a mad dash to clean up and her focus was not on magic but on the club scene. My focus, on the other hand, was on spiritual encounters, especially on a night as powerful and beautiful as this one.

I had waited a long time for Amber to restart the witchcraft classes that would eventually add to our coven. By now, we had a large group of people and were holding our rituals outdoors. A ritual out beneath the moon was something I'd been looking forward to since the festival on the mountain. So why hurry away from the beating drum, the full moon, and the magic, only to go to a club you could patronize any night of the week?

As Amber got ready to leave, she asked me to join them, but I told her I was going home to work on my own magic.

—◊—

On the home front, my relationship with Michael had deteriorated to the point that we were living separate lives under the same roof. One night, he came in from meeting with his counselor and announced that he was voluntarily going back into the hospital and needed me to drive him there.

I did, knowing that the kids came out of hibernation when he was out of the house.

The girls came charging through the back door still wearing their roller blades and racing for the last Popsicle in the freezer. "I got it!" Lynn.

"Not fair." Missy sounded defeated.

The sound of their roller blades were soon overshadowed by the dribbling of a basketball as Aaron came down the stairs. "Going out to shoot a few hoops," he said, passing through the back door.

It was refreshing to see them fearless and carefree. I was able to kick my feet up and relax like an off-duty security guard. Michael's hospital stay was a welcomed vacation. Even though we had one more thing on our to-do list (daily hospital visits), our household seemed to function with much more ease.

Our peace was short-lived, however. All too soon Michael called, saying he was being released and wanted a ride. With his presence, the tension returned to our home.

—m—

I was mentally exhausted, but made sure to cover Luna before retiring to bed. It was an early night for me, and with Michael already asleep on the couch, I climbed in bed with Cujo joining me as my foot warmer. Soon I fell asleep.

I awoke when He came into the room, startled by His captivating face as His deep eyes pierced straight through me. He had dark shoulder-length hair and a mustache and beard, and wore a simple white robe. His radiant countenance consumed me as He spoke six simple words "Who do you say I am?"

I sat straight up in bed, my heart pounding and my body shaking and sweating. I had experienced dreams before that seemed real, but this was the most vivid one I'd ever had. I could still hear His words echoing in my head.

I took a deep breath, trying to calm myself and slow my

breathing. Unsure if I was awake or still dreaming, I turned on the bedroom light and looked around the room. No one was there, but I still felt like I was being watched. I knew that face; I knew that voice. I was used to having dreams, but how would I interpret Jesus appearing to me now? Why would He come and ask that question of me? He had asked a similar question of His disciples long ago, but I wasn't a disciple; I wasn't even a follower.

Some pagans would answer the question by saying He's a prophet or a teacher, while Christians would say He's the Savior. But this was a personal question that had been addressed directly to me as His eyes stared intensely into mine.

Not prepared to answer, I turned the light off and began to drift back to sleep. Before I could, we were face to face once more. "Who do you say I am?" I panicked and reached for the light, my fingers fumbling for the switch. Light filled the room again, and I attempted to calm my racing heartbeat.

"Why won't this dream go away?" I asked aloud. This time I stayed awake a while longer, trying to make sure the dream would end, but when I finally dozed off, I heard the same question a third time. I tossed and turned, trying to drown out His voice, until I finally sat up and shouted, "I don't know—but I'll find out!"

All became quiet, and a peace came into the room. I was able to sleep through the rest of the night, believing that for now He was satisfied with my response.

Over the next six months, I tried to ignore the dream. I didn't want to think about what it might have meant, nor did I want to acknowledge from whom it came. I had actually enjoyed interpreting dreams, seeking to discover their meanings and what their messages held, but this one caused a tremendous disturbance in my spirit. Trying to snuff it out, I continued along my magical path.

I made the mistake of telling Bo about it, and every time I talked with him, he reminded me of the promise I made. I'd always put him off, telling him I would come through in the right timing, but today I felt the guilt of not doing what I had promised.

Questioning why I had made this promise in the first place, I remembered the restless turmoil in my soul as those eyes pierced right through me and the voice posed that question until I vowed to find the answer. No matter how hard I tried to disregard the dream, it remained etched in my memory.

I finally determined that since I wasn't having much success ignoring it, maybe I could disprove it instead. Pastor John knew the Bible and was well aware of my spirituality, so I figured he would know if the dream could have possibly come from Jesus. Once he confirmed there was no way it could have come from God, I could dismiss these thoughts once and for all and get on with my life.

Now unable to remember the number I used to know by heart, I scrambled through a drawer searching for the old church directory. I finally came across an old phone book and made the call.

Pastor John answered the phone and immediately told me that God had brought me to mind and he had been praying for me.

"Tell me it had nothing to do with dreams," I said, still convinced I could dismiss the dream after one conversation with him. "I really just want to ask you about this dream I had a while back."

"A dream? Well, Scripture says sons and daughters will prophesy, old men will dream dreams, and young men will see visions, but you and I both know there's also another source of such dreams."

"Well, this dream seemed so real that it was as if this person was standing right there in my room staring at me. Even when I awoke, it wouldn't go away."

"What was the dream about?" Pastor John asked.

"I dreamt of the face of Jesus, and His eyes seemed to pierce right through me. He spoke only a few words." I went on to explain the question I'd been asked multiple times. "Even awake, I could still see the image of that face and hear those words," I told him. "I've never had a dream like that."

Pastor John's next words surprised me: "Jesus loves you so much that now He's appearing to you in dreams."

"But was that really Jesus? I mean, I'm not exactly one of His followers you know," I pointed out. "Why would He come to me?"

"I don't know, but you're the one who said you saw the face of Jesus, and what was said to you was scriptural, so I don't see any reason to doubt that it was Him. So what did you say to Him?"

"I didn't know what to say, but every time I'd close my eyes to go back to sleep, I'd hear that voice asking me that same question again and again. Finally, I said, 'I don't know—but I'll find out.' Then it all finally stopped."

"Then maybe you ought to find out so you can answer that question," Pastor John suggested. "Maybe you should come back to church and see for yourself."

I sighed. "I couldn't do that even if I wanted to. I was kicked out."

"You weren't kicked out. We told you that you could come back as soon as you had a change of heart," Pastor John reminded me. "I believe God is speaking to you, and if you like, I'll talk with the elders about your coming back as you search for that answer."

Now I was more confused than ever. "I don't know what I want to do, but if I have to promise to have no part in Wicca in order to come back, that's not something I'm willing to do."

"At this point, no one is asking you to do anything," he reassured me, "but you said Jesus appeared to you in a dream, and I believe He's waiting for an answer from you. I imagine you will have no peace until you find a way to answer His question."

I considered that. "Okay. If they say I can come back, I will, but I'm not making any promises. I'm just looking for an answer so I can put this all behind me forever."

"I'll speak with the elders and get back to you."

Pastor John was a man of his word and I knew he would contact the elders, but I was totally confused by this unexpected turn of events. I had expected him to confirm that the dream could not have come from God, let alone Jesus Himself. Not only did he seem convinced otherwise, but he was talking about letting me back in the church doors.

I didn't even know if I wanted to go back there. I was very happy practicing Wicca. Still, I'd made a promise I'd best keep. Why hadn't He just left me alone? Why did I have to have that dream? Was there another logical explanation? I dared not ask my high priestess. How would I explain Jesus showing up in my dreams? *Well*, I thought, *I really have nothing to worry about, because there's no way all the elders will ever agree to me coming back. I might as well get on with my life.*

That meant it was time to prepare for another Yuletide celebration.

—⁓—

The house was decked out in evergreen garland and strings of star lights. We gathered around the Yule tree that was decorated with suns, moons, and stars for ritual and the traditional lighting of the Yule log before opening our exchanged gifts. Since our celebration was open to children, my kids joined Amber's and opened their gifts first.

I looked around the room and realized what a diverse group we were, coming from all walks of life. Our high priest, a former military official, planted himself on the couch as usual, sharing his Shamanistic insight with us. Sequoia, who was exploring her Native American heritage, listened intently as he conveyed his knowledge on purifying one's mind, body, and spirit at sweat lodge ceremonies. Brooke, the optimist of the coven who worked as a secretary, and her husband, Forrester, a professional groundskeeper, were on the loveseat sharing a piece of Yule log cake. We were also joined by some friends who were invited to work with us on occasion.

I turned and found myself staring into a glass of mead that reflected the twinkling lights of the tree. Orion, a soft-spoken Irish man, smiled as he handed me the glass. He made some mean mead, and I always looked forward to his drink of the gods.

I arrived home late as usual and found a note that said Pastor John had called. I wondered what had prompted this call since I had always been the one to initiate contact between us. Then I remembered our discussion about my dream and Pastor John's promise to talk with the eldership about me. He was probably calling to tell me that their biblical standards still wouldn't allow my return.

I could wait until tomorrow to hear the negativity, so I went to bed.

I slept in as late as was possible in my house, not in any hurry to return Pastor John's call and face yet another rejection from my former church family. I called Bo first, but was sorry I did when he enthusiastically encouraged me to call and find out what Pastor John had to say. I finally did, and as I waited for Pastor John to pick up, I pondered what my reaction should be this time when they told me I still wasn't allowed in church. *Why should I even care?* I asked myself.

My thoughts were interrupted by Pastor John's familiar voice.

"I'm sorry I missed your call last night," I said as calmly as I could.

"I'm so glad you called." A hint of excitement tinged his voice. "I spoke with the eldership, and it's all right for you to come back while you search for the answer to His question."

I couldn't believe my ears. "You mean to say they're all okay with this and that I'm actually allowed in church?"

"I'm not going to say it didn't take some deliberation," he said, "but in the end, we all agreed that none of us wanted to stand between Jesus and you, especially when He's showing Himself in your dreams. The eldership is in agreement for you to come."

"What about Pastor Jacob?" I asked, remembering my last conversation with him.

"It was a long evening with a heated discussion. At one point, Pastor Luke's wife came in to check on things after hearing Pastor Jacob slamming his fist down on the table. It certainly wasn't a quick decision, but in the end, everyone, including Pastor Jacob, agreed to allow you back."

"So when am I supposed to start coming?"

"Well, the next service is seven o'clock on Christmas Eve. Why don't you come and bring the children?"

"Christmas Eve?" I asked. "Are you sure you want me there then?"

"What better time for you to come back than on the birthday of our Lord?"

Even though I agreed, I had mixed feelings about the eldership's decision. It felt good that they were no longer going to keep me from entering God's house, yet I was also rather annoyed. Who were they to decide my fate? Who were they to play gatekeeper and determine if I would be allowed to come into the presence of God Almighty or not? Where did they get off treating me like some puppet on a string that was only allowed to go where they directed me? Well, I had cut those strings long ago!

Just as my annoyance level rose to the point where I was ready to forget the whole thing, I experienced a flashback of His face and remembered the voice asking that incisive question. The bottom line was I had promised to get the answer and it had nothing to do with people. They could come or go for all I cared. I needed to get this whole thing resolved, hopefully before the new year began.

—ᴠᴠ—

On Christmas Eve, I took a deep breath and anticipated walking through the doors that had been off limits for many years. If not for the children, I might have turned around and driven away before anyone saw me. But the kids were restless, already out of the car and asking me if we were going in or just going to sit in the parking lot. I opened the church door and ushered the children in.

As we entered, I felt like I had just walked past a "no trespassing" sign. I cautiously looked around, waiting for the guard dogs to come running and chase me away. Instead, the entranceway was warm and inviting, tastefully decorated with Christmas greenery and poinsettias. To my relief, I didn't recognize the greeter who handed me the Christmas Eve program. I steered the children toward some vacant seats in the back, hoping to become just a face in the crowd.

One of the pastors I had not gotten to know very well must have seen us enter and came straight at me with his hand extended. Pastor Luke, who had always seemed to me somewhat conservative, offered me a friendly smile as he shook my hand. Then in a very gentle voice, he spoke my name and said, "I want you to know you're always welcome here."

His words weren't what I expected to hear from him—or from any of the other elders, for that matter. He seemed sincere, and I really didn't know quite how to react. I smiled and thanked him, not wanting to give any indication of the major impact his words had just had on me.

As we settled in our seats, I looked around and recognized only about half of the people. The church had gained a lot of new faces over the years. Someone came alongside me, and as I turned to see who it was, Joan took me in her arms and said how glad she was to see me. I felt like a lost child who had found her way home into the welcome comfort of her mother's embrace.

This pristine moment was quickly marred as she added, "God has so much for you, and He wants so much to pour out His blessing on you. I believe He wants to restore all the years that have been robbed from you by this Wicca or whatever you call it. Just turn from Wicca and back to Him."

A coldness replaced the warmth in her embrace. With anger rising up in me, I braced myself for the words I knew were coming next.

"You've been listening to the lies of Satan. The demons of witchcraft come straight from the pit of hell, but God's truth will prevail."

I pulled back from Joan's hold and tried once more to explain the truth of what I was involved in. "It's not Satan or his demons. You don't understand. Wiccans don't even believe there is a Satan, except perhaps in the warped minds of man."

Joan's face scrunched with frustration. "You have so much to offer in God's kingdom. Don't let the enemy rob that from you. Don't use the gifts God has given for the devil's purpose." Nothing had changed.

I tried one more time. "I don't use anything for some devil's purpose."

Remembering my reason for being there, I determined to concentrate on that and remember that the people were not the issue here. Painting on a grin, I prepared to sit back down.

"We have a gift for you and your family." Joan handed me a nicely wrapped package. "I hope that as you read this, it will help you in some way. God's gift to us is the perfect gift."

I could tell it was some type of book, but before I could say anything more, the first few chords of the guitar silenced the room. As everyone made their way to their seats, Joan gave me a final hug. "I love you."

Relieved the conversation was over, I tried to relax and enjoy all my old favorite Christmas songs. The children presented a small play after worship, then a short message was shared, with the entire service lasting only an hour. People began emptying out of the rows of chairs, and Pastor John came over and greeted me with a warm hug.

"It's great to see you." He smiled at the children and then at me. "We'll be expecting you on Sunday."

At that point, I realized this wasn't just a one-time invitation. The doors were open for my return.

"I'll be here," I said tentatively.

His smile widened. "Have a joyful Christmas."

"Thanks. You too."

As we walked out of the church into the cold night air, I looked at the infinite stars. One star had been a sign in Bethlehem thousands of years ago; the wise men had followed that one star. Then I remembered that *Wicca* means "wise one." Could those who followed the star in the sky, bringing gifts of frankincense, myrrh, and gold, have been witches? I picked up the kids, who had already eaten dinner with their grandparents, so when we got home, I sent them upstairs to get ready for bed.

When we arrived home, I made hot chocolate for my children and allowed them to open their traditional Christmas Eve gift. Afterward, I placed the gift from Joan and John underneath the tree.

"Aren't you going to open it, Mom?" the children asked. "It's Christmas Eve, and you get to open one gift too. Besides, Joan said it was for all of us."

"Okay, we'll open it tonight," I agreed.

Their eager eyes watched my every move as I unwrapped the package.

It was a book titled *The Indescribable Gift*. The children gathered around as I began to read them the story, but it was written more for adults, so they quickly lost interest and went to play. Thinking this might be the answer to my inquisitive mind, I became engrossed in reading an explanatory story of the nativity. I barely lifted my eyes from the book when the children interrupted me and asked to put on some Christmas music.

Within a few moments, soft music broke my concentration: "This, this is Christ the Lord, the babe, the son of Mary."

I closed the book and sat there staring at the tree lights. What child is this? Pagans recognized Him as a prophet, and Christians called Him the Christ. Even the shepherds and angels seemed to know who He was, yet I struggled with the answer. Was He a prophet, a teacher, a god, or all of the above? Dare I include Him as a god and not the Son of God? What about Christ the King, the Savior? Was this some kind of weird game of truth or dare, and if so what would the consequences be if I chose wrongly?

I put the book on the shelf, deciding I had mulled over it enough for tonight.

CHAPTER FIFTEEN

—✺—

I reached over and hit the snooze button, forgetting why I even set the alarm. And then it hit me—it was Sunday morning and the alarm was set so I could get up for church. Early Sunday mornings were my time to catch up on sleep, and the last thing I felt like doing was getting out of my nice, warm bed and getting ready for—of all places—church! I would much prefer a midnight service as I was more accustomed to night hours.

It seemed like only a second had passed when the buzz angered me all over again. This was it. I had to crawl out from beneath my covers and spend the next fifteen minutes coaxing the kids out from under theirs. I asked myself why a witch would be showering for church instead of shutting off the alarm and going back to sleep. Of course, I knew the answer, but I didn't want to think about it, so the best thing to do was follow through on the whole church thing.

I opened my closet to an array of black clothing, from a velvet dress to black leggings and black boots. I had only a witchy wardrobe, with absolutely nothing that would truly be considered appropriate for church. I finally settled on black velvet stretch pants and a black tie-dyed velvet tunic. I laced up my black boots, threw my cape on, and gathered the children, realizing for the first time that my attire was a definite fashion statement of my mind-set.

At church, we found seats in the back row near the exit. Pastor John and Joan came over to offer a warm welcome, and seconds later, a couple got up and found other seats. More people did the same. I didn't know if it was my black attire or the rumors of witchcraft, but their swift exit resulted in an evacuation of our row. As we sat there, I realized I dressed more like Stevie Nicks than Joyce Meyer. I felt like a misfit and didn't really know if I wanted to fit in.

Worship then began. The songs were all new to me, but the clapping and dancing that had been subdued on Christmas Eve returned. All the children were in the front of the church with a few women leading them in song and dance, reminding me of how my kids used to dance in the back.

Things were pretty much the same as I remembered. When the time came for communion, I declined the cup and bread, as I had become accustomed to cakes and ale with my coven. Once again I asked what I was doing here, but Pastor John was about to start teaching, so it was too late for a graceful exit.

It had been a long time since I sat through a teaching, and I found it hard to concentrate. I was used to taking a more active part in things, so my mind started to quickly wander. No wonder people found Christianity so boring. There was nothing to do but become a spectator for two hours and listen to what somebody else had learned from reading the Scriptures. The service finally ended, and we left as quickly as we could get out the door.

Why did my promise have to be so complicated?

—⁂—

One evening, Michael came home early from work and announced, "I've got bad news." He looked so downhearted that I thought someone had died.

"What's wrong?" I asked.

"The plant is closing and I'm out of a job."

I tried to remain calm. "When are they closing?"

"We have one month, and then I'll collect some severance pay before we have nothing." Michael then retreated upstairs to his asylum of sleep, and I was left scrambling to figure out how to keep food on the table and a roof over my children's heads.

His layoff was an extremely stressful time, and Michael spent the time in bed or glued to his computer, which didn't help. He grew angrier every day and made no effort to look for another job. I grew concerned when I heard him yell, "You no good piece of crap!" and entered the room to find him chucking the keyboard to the floor.

I doubted he was on his meds, so I went to check the medicine cabinet. The bottle should have been close to empty, but it was full.

Then Tuesday night went by and Michael didn't go to his counseling appointment. When I asked why, he barked, "I don't have the money to go." I thought his answer rather strange since he was supposedly going for free.

And then there was Bo, who said he wanted a real relationship with me. I had some reservations about committing to a divorce from Michael and a remarriage to Bo—who wanted me to move clear across the country to a house he had built for us. My first priority was my children, and I didn't want to take them so far away from the family they had grown up around.

I also couldn't help but question Bo's motive for moving me clear across the country. Did he just want to get me away from my coven, thinking that would end my spiritual quest? He was already showing signs of wanting to control my life and even choose my friends. He assured me there was a whole new group of friends waiting for me near his desert home—all of whom were Christian, of course.

The coven, on the other hand, was in a slump, which actually worked in my favor. Amber was still exhibiting "maiden energy," as she called it, and wasn't focused on magic. Rituals were being planned and canceled or not planned at all. I understood she needed some time to have the fun she'd always felt deprived of in her youth, but while she was hitting the clubs, I was looking for an answer. With rituals few and far between, I had the perfect opportunity for my quest.

However, I was finding the whole church thing a lot harder than I thought it would be. I didn't really want to be there, and was determined to remain distant from the body to avoid any further hurt when the shunning resumed. After all, I still hadn't recovered from the wounds inflicted from their last rejection. Pastor John kept encouraging me to not go to rituals and to discontinue my relationship with coveners, but I reminded him that was not part of our agreement. I was a witch in search of Jesus, and even if I did decide to stay, the one thing I made perfectly clear was that I would not shun my pagan friends as the church had shunned me.

I did read a little book Joan had given me. It was about a child's relationship with God outside the whole church scene, which I could relate to. A simple, childlike relationship with the Father was appealing to me. If nothing else, the book was uncomplicated.

I wished my life could be as simple.

One morning while I was still in a semi-conscious, dreamy state, I saw before me a newsletter with some kind of cartoon-like drawing on it. At the top it read, *The Last Days Newsletter*. It seemed familiar, but I couldn't place where I had seen it before. I lay there with my eyes wide open, allowing my mind to absorb what I had seen, and then a name came to me—Keith Green. He had played contemporary Christian music and ran a ministry that published *The Last Days Newsletter*.

Years ago, Keith Green had been one of my favorite Christian music artists. But as I tried to think of one of his songs, my mind drew a blank. I felt like I was beating my head against a brick wall as I tried to remember a line from a song or a melody, but absolutely nothing came to mind. How could I have forgotten songs I had listened to daily for years? It didn't make sense. How could I remember "Puff the Magic Dragon" from my childhood, but the Christian music that once had such an impact on me was wiped from my memory?

I picked up the kids, who had already eaten dinner with their grandparents, so when we got home, I sent them upstairs to get ready for bed.

I called a few of the pastors. Pastor Jacob said he had some of Keith Green's music around somewhere, along with a book about him, and he'd try to find them. The urgency I felt compelled me to go to a Christian bookstore not far from home and see what I could find on my own.

I felt rather strange walking into a Christian bookstore after all this time. I hurried past the shelves of books and Bibles and found my way around to the music section. A whole new generation of Christian musicians had come about, and I didn't recognize any of their names. As I wondered if there were any artists there I would remember, I found two double CD sets of Keith Green's music. I didn't have enough money to buy both, so I decided on *The Ministry Years*.

The adrenaline rush of the hunt then subsided, and I remembered what I was and where I was. I was a witch in a Christian bookstore buying Christian music. I hesitated when they asked for my address to put on their mailing list, then gave them my husband's name and swiftly made my way out the door.

Still feeling an urgency to discover the meaning behind my dream, I put the CD in the car's player. As Keith Green sang "How Can They Live Without Jesus," all the words I once knew by heart came flooding back to me. I drove home with tears running down my cheeks. Memories of how much this music had once moved me and how those newsletters always seemed to be a confirmation of what God was doing in my own life filled my mind. I didn't know how something that had been so much a part of my life could have been so completely suppressed in my memory. As I listened to the next song, "You Can Run to the End of the Highway," I thought that it could have been written just for me.

When I got home, I rushed inside and put the CD in the player in our living room. The words penetrated deep into my spirit, reminding me that nothing that I've done remains. Then it hit me. Even after all I'd done and all I had become, God still saw no stain on me. This music had once had an impact on my life, but now it took on an entirely new meaning, more than I could ever have imagined.

I listened to every song, and each one brought back something that I had lost along the way. The stirring inside me intensified, and I realized the dream of that newsletter had led me right to this music.

I was so excited about what was happening that I had to share it with somebody. I called Bo and told him all about the dream and how I had even driven to the Christian bookstore, unable to wait for Pastor Jacob to find his CDs. Bo sounded as excited as I was as I told him how even the very first song I listened to not only unlocked memories but also uncovered my eyes and opened my ears to what God was trying to say. I had stumbled upon a way to answer the question Jesus had asked me.

Pastor Jacob never did find his CDs, but he did loan me the book about Keith Green's life. Bo sent me the other set of Keith Green's music, which I wasted no time immersing myself in it. The lyrics of one song declared how nothing lasts except for the grace of God, and that's when I recognized that it's all about God's grace. Then I heard the words to the song that had always moved me at Pastor Jacob's prayer meetings, "Create in Me a Clean Heart." I had never realized it was a Keith Green song, but today it had renewed significance.

I couldn't wait to read the book about Keith Green's life, music, and ministry. It took me back to that time in my life when so much of his music seemed to reflect what I felt I was hearing from God. But when I got to the part of the book where Keith and eleven others were killed in a plane crash, I remembered how devastated I had been and realized that I had never really dealt with the questions and the anger it had caused within me. I asked the same questions I had asked back then, and seemed no closer to finding the answers than I had many years ago.

What had happened? Was the crash the result of a spiritual

attack? Keith Green's ministry and music had greatly impacted my life, and I couldn't handle the possibility that dark forces had been able to destroy it. I had been part of a church with a ministry of healing and deliverance, so I was very aware of spiritual warfare. If Keith Green could be struck down, how would I be able to withstand such an attack?

When we had moved, I never sent his ministry my change of address, so I never received another newsletter or the answers to my questions. Reading the book about Keith Green's life and death had rekindled the fear that I had hidden away so deep inside that I didn't realize it still existed. I had to deal with it now, so I picked up the phone and called Pastor John.

I told him how listening to the songs had helped me remember so many things I had forgotten, and shared my concerns about the tragic plane crash. "When I got to the part in the book about the plane crash, I realized I had never really dealt with it," I explained. "I find myself asking the same questions I asked back then, like, where was God's protection for him?"

"If I remember correctly," Pastor John said, "they had way too many people on the plane, right?"

"Yes, it did say that. But God was using Keith to reach so many people. Why would He allow such a tragedy to happen?"

"God does protect us," he gently explained, "but the Bible also says we are not to tempt Him by stepping out from under His covering. I don't know what happened that moment with Keith, but you have to trust that God had him in His care. Look at how his legacy is still having an impact for the kingdom today."

"But it's frightening to think this man who knew God, who moved in the Spirit, who God was using mightily in his ministry, took one step out from under God's covering and the next minute his plane crashed to the ground," I pointed out. "It's unrealistic to think one will never step out from under God's covering, and some devil is just hanging around waiting for that time someone slips up and slam, that's it?"

"Wait a minute here," he said. "We don't know all that happened leading up to that day. For example, did God tell him not to go? Did Keith even ask if he should be going? Only God knows all those details, but two things we do know are that he is now with the Lord and God used even that situation to reach a lot of people. It seems it has really impacted your life."

"I guess I hadn't realized just how much it impacted me until today."

"God does protect His people," he assured me. "There is no reason to fear. Fear is not of God."

Was that really true? And even if it was, where did I stand with all of this? I certainly was out from under God's protective covering, according to what Pastor John and all the other pastors had been telling me. For a moment, I was struck with fear that only added to my dilemma.

And I still hadn't answered the question Jesus had asked.

CHAPTER SIXTEEN

—ᘑᘏ—

I stood in the corridor outside what appeared to be an elegant ballroom. Before me were two enormous wooden doors, carved with intricate designs and rounded on the top to form an arched doorway. The doors stood ajar, and they were much thicker than any earthly door I'd ever seen.

I peered through them into a massive, spectacular room. Thousands of people sang in adoration and joyous celebration, creating a warm and inviting atmosphere. On the far right were angels—beings with featureless faces and an intense inner light that radiated through the multitude of lucid wings surrounding a throne that rose high above. I was mesmerized, overcome by fear, and dared not enter—though the idea enticed me.

Suddenly, I stared into darkness, too petrified to move. Had I just witnessed the throne room of God Almighty? Even though I was now awake, the multitudes in the ballroom terrified me. My mind could hardly comprehend this glimpse of eternity, where angels gathered around God's throne. Surely this place was off limits, yet why was the door open as if to court my entry? I lay there staring at the ceiling, with Cujo snuggled next to me, for what seemed an eternity itself until my eyelids grew heavy and I couldn't keep them open any longer.

I felt small and insignificant outside of the arched doorway. The door was wide open, but the room was empty. After gathering enough courage to enter, I was surrounded by an enormous ballroom with a cathedral ceiling and finely crafted decorative walls. Large pillars were evenly positioned around the outer edge of the room, which was void of any furniture. I stood on a floor of smooth stone, situated near the door in case I needed to flee.

When all seemed safe, I walked around the room, admiring the artwork on the walls. On the far side of the room, I stopped, sensing His presence at the door. I ran to the corner and cowered like a frightened puppy with its tail between its legs, but this presence was non-threatening and waited patiently by the door.

I felt reassured that I wasn't in harm's way, and an enormous sense of peace rested on me. After uncurling myself, I took a few steps toward the center of the room. Then His all-consuming presence entered the room, sending me back to the corner. Shaking, I attempted to hide. He didn't speak a word or confront me. Instead, He slowly came to the center of the room and sat in the only seat that now occupied the room, waiting.

My fear subsided and I felt safe. He threw something to me—a silver ball—but I let it roll away. He waited for me to realize it was safe to play, then threw the ball again and I caught it. His presence was soothing, and eventually I threw the ball back. The game had begun.

The great room became a warm and comfortable place. I now had nothing to fear, not the room and not His presence in it. Then He called me to Him, but I looked away, afraid to get close and afraid to see His face. I was reminded that no harm would come to me, that it was okay. Trembling, I moved closer, each step seeming endless as I approached His feet. I sat like a child at the feet of her Father, receiving these words of encouragement: "Climb onto the lap of your Father, for it is here you will find comfort and here where you will be safe."

Sunlight broke through the closed curtains and brightened my bedroom. Slipping from sleep to consciousness, I thought about the marvelous great room and wondered if it was the temple of the living God. Would He really allow me in, play with me until He won my trust, and even call me to climb up on His knee? Would God still consider me His child after all I had done? Did I even have a right to consider Him Abba Father, coming from where I'd been? I had to find out what all of this meant, so I called Pastor John and shared my dream with him. As we spoke, our other phone line rang.

"Go ahead and answer it," he said. "We both know who it is."

It was indeed Amber, needing to discuss some things with me. I told her I'd call her back and returned to my conversation with Pastor John, anxious to hear what he had to say about my dream. We had spent a lot of time talking about my dreams lately.

He asked, "Don't you think it's ironic that just as you're telling me about yet another way God is revealing Himself to you, you get a call from your high priestess?"

"Well, maybe. But we do talk a lot." I wondered what difference it made. "More likely it's just coincidence."

"Even if it is coincidence, it reminds me that there's something I want to discuss with you. A while back we talked about praying for your deliverance, and I think it's time we do that."

"When I first came to New Zion, I had prayer for deliverance," I reminded him.

"True," he said, "but that was before you became involved in the occult and opened yourself to demonic influences. I think it's time to get rid of them."

Here we go again. "It's true that I haven't been following Jesus, but it doesn't have anything to do with demons," I insisted.

He sighed. "Well, I see you're still in denial. Let me know when you want to be healed."

I knew all too well what deliverance was about. I'd have to confess to a list of things they felt had demons attached to them and then remove them from my life—things like Wicca, the Goddess, and magic. But I didn't think these things were demonic, and I didn't want prayer to get rid of them. All I wanted was to find out who Jesus was. My being there in the church had nothing to do with chasing out demons. Why couldn't we just stick to who Jesus was and stop bringing up unrelated subjects all the time?

—⚏—

Our Thursday prayer meeting was now being held in the home of one of the newest deacons. His family had been attending the church for quite some time, though I'd never met them before. They certainly had a knack for hospitality, and I felt welcomed as soon as I walked in the door.

Pastor John and Joan were there to oversee the meeting, which went pretty much the way I remembered. When it came time for the group to pray for one another, I didn't raise my hand, but the next thing I knew I had several people laying hands on me. I could deal with their praying for me as long as they didn't expect me to denounce any of my involvement in the Craft.

After the meeting ended, Joan approached me. "How are things with you and Michael?" she asked.

"We're more like roommates than a married couple, and now the pressure is on me to provide since he's unable to work and filed for disability," I explained.

"That's a shame. I remember Michael's heart toward you and the desire of your heart." She shook her head sadly. "Why isn't he able to work?"

"They closed the plant and he fell further into depression, so hopefully the disability will be approved." I took a deep breath. "At one time, I wanted nothing more than a loving marriage, but there's no chance of that now."

"God can heal Michael and bring new life to your marriage," she encouraged me, "but you've dabbled in things of the enemy, who wants to destroy the relationship between you and Michael."

My defenses went up. My relationship with Michael had been over long before I became involved with witchcraft. You can't blame my failing marriage on witchcraft."

"Let's just pray," she said. "I know God would like nothing better than to give you the desires of your heart that have been robbed from you." She then motioned for a few of the other women to come and pray with us.

I sat on a chair in the middle of the room as the women gathered around and laid hands on me. I tried to concentrate on the prayer going forth but instead attempted to contain the anger I felt. How dare Joan blame my marital problems on my spiritual path! Had she forgotten my trouble with Michael began when I was a Christian trying to walk a godly life?

I kept my eyes closed and bit my tongue, all the while wanting to scream, "All the praying in the world didn't save my marriage, and I doubt it will restore it now!"

CHAPTER SEVENTEEN

—⁓—

B efore me I saw a translucent white opal freestanding stairway that led toward heaven. The open risers gave a clear view of the blue-sky oasis on the other side, while banisters of angels lined the rails. I was directed to the base of the stairs, where they showed me the openings between steps. The stair treads had a slippery sheen, and a voice instructed, "Take one step at a time. Do not move to the next without completing the one you're on."

I had the sense that each step represented an obstacle to overcome. "Beware of skipping a step, for you surely will fall." I felt myself sliding through the riser opening and realized it was symbolic for the warning I've been given: "Do not listen to those who would have you miss a step, no matter what they say."

I opened my eyes to the sound of a loud bell, and for a moment didn't know where I was. The bus was empty, but the sound of the children's footsteps and voices became increasingly louder. Where had the time gone? I started the bus and opened the door. After checking my watch, I glanced at my route schedule. It all seemed so irrelevant compared to what I had just dreamt while I was awake.

—⁓—

My quest for answers still not satisfied. I continued to get up on Sunday mornings and go to church, as well as faithfully attend Thursday-night prayer meetings, though I struggled with the structured format and with Christians I couldn't relate to. I felt like a foreigner in some strange land, unfamiliar with the language and having no desire to conform to their dress code. Where was God among the men in suits and woman dressed to the hilt in this house of worship?

Where were the passionate Jesus freaks? Where was the entry-level church—the one you could walk into with muddy feet and be welcomed no matter what you looked like or how you were dressed? There was such a drastic difference between the land from which I'd come and where I was now. I thought about the simple child's book I had read, longing for a simple relationship with the Father.

While battling all these conflicting questions, I came across Hebrews 6:4–6: "For it is impossible for those who were once enlightened, and have tasted the heavenly gift, and have become partakers of the Holy Spirit, and have tasted the good word of God and the powers of the age to come, if they fall away, to renew them again to repentance, since they crucify again for themselves the Son of God, and put Him to an open shame" (NKJV).

There before me were the very words the born-agains had spoken to me outside Cerridwen's Cauldron. Was I doomed for all eternity? I had known Jesus—had tasted the heavenly gifts—and I became a witch. Maybe the born-again outside the shop was right and I was wasting my time. I picked up the phone and called Pastor Jacob.

"I read in Hebrews that if you've known God and have turned away, you can't come back," I said. "Is that true about me?"

"I believe this Scripture is speaking of a person who has gone so far from God that they no longer have any remorse," he explained. "Their hearts have become completely hardened to the things of God. I don't believe this Scripture is describing you."

"Why not?" Really, it sounded exactly like me.

"If you had come to a place of total rejection of God, I wouldn't be having this conversation with you. The fact that you're concerned about this and talking with me about it proves you haven't completely rejected God. Believe me, the elders have already prayed about this. No one feels you have reached the point of no return."

I considered that. "I don't know. You don't know me. You don't know my heart."

"I know enough," he said, "and I believe this is just another lie from Satan to try and deceive you into thinking that there's no point in trying."

As we concluded our conversation, I wasn't so sure that I agreed with Pastor Jacob's assessment. The Scripture seemed to fit me to a tee. I kept hearing that guy at the shop telling me how I'd burn in the fiery pit of hell forever, but it seemed liked I was already living it right here on earth.

Would I ever sort this all out? And was there any point in really trying? Everywhere I turned, I found more questions than answers.

—⚏—

Amber called to say it had been too long since we had a circle so she was planning a ritual for Friday night and expected me there before everyone else to help with preparations. I looked forward to it, and shared my plans with Bo, which I always did.

"You can't do that!" he exclaimed.

"Excuse me?" I said. "Who are you to tell me what I can and can't do?"

"How can you still go after the dreams and all the ways God's been speaking to you?"

"Yeah, but I didn't hear Him say not to go to a ritual," I pointed out. "It's you that's trying to control me, and I don't like being controlled!"

"But it's like you're cheating on God. I'm calling Pastor John."

"Go right ahead," I said. "As a matter of fact, I'll call him for you."

My conversation with Pastor John wasn't nearly as hostile as the one with Bo, but it brought us to another issue that never seemed far below the surface. "You know it's really not the best timing for you to go to a ritual," he said calmly. "Why not tell the high priestess and the others that you aren't going to be around for a while. Take a sabbatical. Give God a chance."

"I am giving God a chance. Isn't that what I have been doing? But I'm not going to turn my back on my friends, because I know what that feels like. Besides, when Michael was hospitalized and my family was in crisis, they were there for me. While you may not agree with them spiritually, they didn't forsake me like you and God did."

"I can understand you not wanting to turn your back on these people who have been there for you. I'm sure they've had the best intentions concerning your well-being, but the blind can't lead the blind. Let's set a time for prayer."

I knew where this was going. "You mean deliverance. I don't need deliverance."

"What do you enjoy about demons?" he asked.

"Well, at least they welcome me to their meetings! Come on, Pastor John, don't be ridiculous. This isn't Scooby-Doo!" I told him for probably the hundredth time.

"Well, then praying shouldn't be a problem. Let's just pray and get it over with."

Realizing this was going to be an ongoing battle if I didn't agree to something, I asked jokingly, "And who would be there for my exorcism?"

"Joan, myself, and some of the others from the healing team." He then suggested a time and place to meet.

As we hung up, I realized I had agreed to meet for them to pray and deliver me from the evil they thought I was involved in. How in the world had I let it go that far?

—◈—

Still determined to attend ritual, I dropped my kids off at their grandparents' house and drove to the long, winding mountain road to The Village. Amber had already closed the shop, so we had a glass of wine and talked about the full moon ritual while waiting for the others.

Drums beat in time with the shadows of flames dancing on the wall as Orion smudged us and I used Sabbat oil to anoint each covener. Amber cast the magic circle, others were assigned to call quarters, and I again called the Guardians of the West. Once sacred space was created and Amber invoked the Goddess, she walked about the circle prophesying to us and gave everyone a Goddess amulet as a symbol of her gift that night. We then partook of cakes and ale or bread and mead before closing the circle with the chant, "Merry do we meet, merry do we part to merry meet again."

A potluck feast awaited us as we gathered together like family to debrief. With the lights on, we now could see the amulets that had been given us. On mine was the image of a goddess sitting behind a large comb. It symbolized self-reliance, exactly what I would need in facing the challenges ahead in my life.

As was often the case, it was very late by the time I picked up the kids and got home. No sooner had I walked in the door when the phone rang.

Bo, enraged that I had gone to ritual in spite of his objections, was on the other end of the line. "About time you got home! It's the middle of the night!" he screamed at me. "You shouldn't be out late like this. What am I to think?"

"You don't need to think anything. I already told you I was going to a ritual," I reminded him.

"It's not good, cheating on God like that! I know what kind of things go on there." Bo's response really irritated me, like he really knew what went on at a ritual.

"What are you accusing me of?" I challenged. "All you know are your preconceived ideas!" This conversation reminded me of countless others I'd had with Pastor John and Michael over the years. I had thought Bo was different, and found myself uncomfortable with where this was heading.

"God is a jealous God!"

Bo had become the typical Christian man I'd come to resent. How dare he use God as his scapegoat. His issue with this had more to do with my being at a ritual with pagan men, and his own jealousy because of his belief about what went on during ritual.

"Don't use God as an excuse for your own insecurities!" I shouted, and not wanting to continue the argument, I hung up. His double-standard aggravated me, and I couldn't take his eagerness to quote Scripture that benefited only him.

—⁂—

I finally agreed to submit to the church leadership for prayer for deliverance, not because I really wanted it or felt it was needed, but because they were so insistent. The evening came and I arrived at Pastor John and Joan's house. After a brief explanation of what would happen, they prayed for me, covering a laundry list of demonic influences. I went along with them, although mentally rejecting the list of seemingly harmless things they were concerned about.

In the past, when people had prayed for my deliverance, I really felt as though something was happening. This time I felt nothing at all. At one point, I was asked to stand, remove my black cape, and take a few steps away from it, signifying a leaving behind of the darkness and a walking into the light. As I walked the few steps, I heard, "I am still here," but choose to keep the message to myself. Before I left, they handed me written instructions for walking out my deliverance. I picked up my belongings, including my spiritual homework, and threw on my black cape before heading home.

For the next week or so, the members of the deliverance team called often to see if I needed prayer. They would always ask if I was feeling the results of the deliverance, but I was never convinced there were any demons to pray against, so what difference could I really expect?

I continued going to church and prayer meetings, reading Scripture, and trying to figure out who Jesus was. I also continued going to rituals, though I refrained from any personal magical workings. Both God and the Goddess were still having a significant impact on my life, and I couldn't see why I needed to give up one for the other. There was plenty of room in my life for both. I also couldn't accept the biblical teachings of witchcraft being evil, for I had only experienced good.

I found myself asking who really had an issue with it—God or man?

A WITCH'S ENCOUNTER WITH GOD

CHAPTER EIGHTEEN

—∿—

I wasn't prepared to meet the unfair conditions that New Zion's elders suddenly set before me. I was to have no phone, email, or personal contact with Bo so I could give full devotion to Michael and ask for his forgiveness for my part of the deterioration of our marriage. I didn't know what to make of it; after all, I wasn't part of the church.

The thought of having no contact with Bo seemed devastating. How many times had he been the only one bringing any element of God into my life? And what would Bo think? How would he react to the elders' demands that I stay out of touch with him while I waited to see if God brought restoration to my marriage? Pastor John assured me that if Bo was the man of God that he claimed to be, he would agree to step back and see what God would do—and that if Bo and I were really supposed to be together, he could trust God to bring it about in a godly way.

Pastor John, anticipating my reluctance in this, said he wanted me to put every effort into trying to reestablish a relationship with Michael, no matter how unfair it seemed. He explained that he knew I had already been through a lot, so if things didn't improve after I had submitted to their instructions for the next three months, then the eldership would agree that divorce was acceptable. I thought that strange. Why would I need their approval if I choose to divorce Michael?

I finally agreed to their terms for the sake of appeasing my spiritual dad. I understood his desire to rekindle my marriage since he had invested so much into making it work. Bo determined that he wouldn't go against the elders, although he certainly wasn't in agreement with their reasoning. He acquiesced to reduce our contact to a weekly phone call and promised there would be no romantic conversation, which was to begin the first of March.

Along with the March winds, a great loneliness blew into my life. I struggled not to pick up the phone and call Bo. In a desperate attempt to remain steadfast in not contacting him, I wrote emails but never sent them. I still thought about him often, wondering where he was and what he was doing. I felt all alone, voluntarily sentenced to solitary confinement, as I cried and pleaded with God about my unjust fate. But there was no undoing my pain. All my hopes and dreams seemed to have vanished before my very eyes; only my children brought any sense of joy to my life. I threw all my energy into them and the smiles they gave me.

Late one afternoon, I walked into the kitchen to find Michael making himself a sandwich. Thinking it was as good a time as any to have a heart-to-heart conversation, I began, "I want to talk with you about our marriage."

He dropped the knife, barely missing his foot. Then he turned and listened.

"I'm sorry that I misled you into believing I would always remain a Christian," I said. "I mean, I didn't mean to mislead you; I just surprised myself. And I know I haven't been exactly honest and faithful to you, even involving myself with someone else. I just never thought you cared."

"I know you never intended for this to happen, and neither did I." Not only was Michael speaking to me, but his brown eyes were teary. "I never wanted to hurt you and the kids. I didn't know I was bipolar, and if I'd known, I never would've made you go through all this."

Now I was crying too. "I had hoped after your diagnoses that we could've worked it out, but your counselor said you didn't want me involved." He shook his head. "She told me there would have been more hope for me if I'd gotten help years ago. There was nothing I could do, and our marriage is ruined because of it."

For the first time in years, we hugged, red-eyed and solemn.

Getting this all out in the open brought a sense of relief, but that was where it ended. Nothing changed. There were no sparks left and no rekindling of a fire that had been extinguished a long time ago. Michael never said another word about it, instead retreating within himself to his reclusive world.

A WITCH'S ENCOUNTER WITH GOD

CHAPTER NINETEEN

—〰—

O ur marriage was clearly over, but we didn't have the money to proceed with divorce.

Bo requested a job transfer to be closer, and the next thing I knew he was on his way. His move was bittersweet because, although I had kept my part of the bargain with the elders, I was living in sin if I continued a relationship with him while still legally married.

Several more months went by before Pastor John gave me the ultimatum to divorce Michael immediately or never see Bo again. Ending a relationship with someone who cared about me in exchange for someone who didn't made no sense to me. How could this be God's will for me? Was He a judgmental God who found joy in seeing me suffer? It just didn't seem right. After all, He was the Father who played ball with me in the middle of His throne room and lovingly sat me upon His knee.

I pleaded with Pastor John to hear my heart in the matter. I was taking steps and, while they were small, I was still moving forward. I shared the warnings I had in the dream ("Beware of skipping a step, for you surely will fall," and "Do not listen to those who would have you miss a step, no matter what they say"), but he didn't listen, remaining firm that the relationship needed to end or I would be excommunicated.

"Please, John, not Matthew 18 again," I pleaded. I was so close. If only he would give me more time.

When I told Bo, he was furious. He arranged to speak with Pastor John and Pastor Lyndon, one of the younger members of the pastoral staff. Bo, though not denying the relationship as sinful according to the Bible, asked for grace and compassion as we made the situation right before God over time. He also appealed on my behalf, stating he felt an excommunication would be detrimental to my spiritual well-being.

His requests were met with opposition. They held fast to the Scripture that pertained to "the appearance of evil" that could not be overlooked. As far as my spiritual well-being, they felt that was my choice since I was refusing to follow the authority of their counsel. Their conclusion remained the same: either all communication was to end or I was to be shunned.

I tried speaking with Pastor John one more time, but to my dismay, he not only used my relationship with Bo in their reasoning but brought up a whole list of things they felt I had refused to do in compliance with their instructions. He pointed out that I continued in relationships with my coven members and went to rituals.

Of course I still went to rituals. Had he forgotten the reason I came back to church was to find out who Jesus was? I'd never promised to stop attending rituals, and I certainly had no intention of turning my back on my coven. When did this become a requirement? After all, He was the one who told me to come back to church; I only told him about Jesus showing up in my dream. I thought God was a just God and these men spoke with His authority, so why did this seem so unjust?

Several weeks went by without a word from Pastor John, and I was unsure of where I stood, so I wrote a letter to the elders. I questioned if Matthew 18 was again being applied in my life and asked them to reconsider and extend grace. I also expressed my desire to continue walking toward righteousness and admitted that I had a long way to go. I didn't make excuses for my wrongdoings but asked for time to get it right. Finally, I closed by saying that I knew, since God had sent His Son to a sinful generation, He also possessed the heart of a father reaching out to a lost and wayward one like me to be returned to the fold.

Along with the letter, I sent several songs I felt expressed

God's heart on the matter, one of which was a Keith Green song, "Asleep in the Light," which challenges one's heart to see Jesus in the lost and to recognize that, when you close the door on them, you've left Him out on the street.

I also included a page from *The Ragamuffin Gospel: Good News for the Bedraggled, Beat-Up, and Burnt-Out,* by Brennan Manning, which seemed to me to speak very clearly of this issue:

Any church that will not accept that it consists of sinful men and women, and exists for them, implicitly rejects the gospel of grace. As Hans Kung says, "It deserves neither God's mercy nor men's trust. The church must constantly be aware that its faith is weak, its knowledge dim, its profession of faith halting, that there is not a single sin or failing which it has not in one way or another been guilty of. And though it is true that the church must always dissociate from sin, it can never have any excuse for keeping any sinners at a distance. If the church remains self-righteously aloof from failures, irreligious and immoral people, it cannot enter justified into God's kingdom. But if it is constantly aware of its guilt and sin, it can live in joyous awareness of forgiveness. The promise has been given to it that anyone who humbles himself will be exalted."

Within two weeks, I received a letter from Pastor John on behalf of the eldership. It read:

Thank you for your letters and songs to all the Elders. We all read the note and listened to the lyrics. We believe we understand the point you are making, i.e., the Church and its leadership should somehow be able to embrace those seeking a way back to God, or those who feel outside of the fellowship of the Lord. From the lyrics to the songs, there is implication that while Jesus died on the cross for the lost, Church leadership won't get off their backsides to reach out.

Since our history with you is filled with scores of examples of our abiding love for you, Michael, and your children, we must assume we were not included in the callous leadership not willing to go the extra mile. We recall countless hours of support, prayer, and counseling with you.

Our differences appear to rest on two issues:

1. Acceptance of biblical commands regarding the "appearance of evil," and

2. The eldership's collegial authority

Our hearts are at peace in that we did our part to help you reconcile to the Father who loves you so much. You were welcomed into our prayer meetings, worship, and hearts. You seem to want to follow your own desire to return to pagan meetings and rituals, and continue to fellowship with whomever you think is appropriate. You rejected the counsel and scriptural admonition of our Elders.

Perhaps one day we will have a meeting for people who are searching for spiritual reality, or seeking understanding of the Christian lifestyle, without having to commit to follow the Bible's teachings. That day is not here, and we carry the Lord's commands regarding the lifestyles of the church members very seriously.

Our prayer is for the swift resolution of your life circumstances, for your peace and the full restoration of your fellowship with those who love you. You will remain in our prayers.

Your brother in the Lord,

Pastor John (for the elders)

I didn't quite know how to interpret their letter. It seemed they were missing a very important part. I never said they hadn't offered countless hours of prayer and counseling for me, but rather that so much more was still needed. They seemed to overlook that I was making some progress, and instead claimed I rejected their counsel and didn't adhere to their church standards, but I never said I was a member.

Still unsure if I was being excommunicated or not, I called Pastor John and told him I had received the letter but still didn't understand where I stood. He said he thought it was clearly stated that I could not return until I committed to ending my relationship with Bo and my involvement in witchcraft.

"This is not easy," he said sadly. "You're like a daughter to us, but the elders have decided." His words made me wonder if he didn't completely agree with their decision. "This is only a temporary thing. As soon as you take care of these things, we will gladly restore you into the fellowship."

Letting loose with all my pent-up anger, I screamed "No, it is not temporary! This time, it's definitely permanent! I will never walk into your church again! Thanks for all your countless hours of counsel. Goodbye!"

I hung up the phone, deeply wounded and unable to comprehend how they could view forbidding someone from coming to church as the godly way to handle any situation. I called Bo, who tried to comfort me, but nothing he could say would take away the hurt I was feeling. They had invited me back after I had the dream of Jesus, but now they were discarding me like a piece of garbage. I cried and screamed, and I knew God still loved me, but try as I might I couldn't make any sense of it.

Bo let me vent my anger and then tried to calm me down. "They're just people, and people make mistakes," he said. "God hasn't rejected you just because this one church has. There are many more churches that don't believe in doing things this way. Why don't you try another church?"

"Why should I put myself through this all over again?" I asked. "No way"

"Please try. God has not abandoned you."

"I know God hasn't abandoned me," I assured him. "I know the difference between God and the church, and I'm not giving up on God, but His so-called followers are another thing!"

"Just think about it. You know you need the support of the

church in order to keep going in your walk."

I felt like an aborted baby being severed from its mother's body. Like that unborn child, I had made a desperate attempt to remain safe and secure in an environment that didn't want me.

—ᘚ—

Bo took it upon himself to contact a pastor from a Vineyard church he used to attend. He gave me the email address of Pastor Jeff and told me he had explained the situation to him and that Pastor Jeff would be more than happy to correspond with me through email.

I wrote and introduced myself, giving him a brief summary of my involvement in witchcraft, my church rejection, and my amazing revelation—that God never left me. He soon replied:

> Dear Ally,
>
> What great grace you are experiencing! Many times the church falls short of God's grace, sometimes egregiously, other times just because of our humanity. It's a wonderful and unfortunately rare thing to experience the wisdom and grace that God has for us from one single source. Many times He will use unexpected sources to point us back to Him and find our hope in Him alone. It sounds like you are on such a course. Of course, the enemy wants to keep you isolated and disconnected, so he will use various means to accomplish that. Unfortunately, the church cooperates all too readily, but then again sometimes we're coming from the darkness of our own perspective or our expectation is faulty—oftentimes it's a combination. The main point, put your trust in God, His grace, and connect with His people the best you can (read cautiously) because sinners need each other. Thanks for writing and I'm glad our teachings are a help to you in your journey.
>
> Jeff

So began my communication with Pastor Jeff. Bo arranged to have the church's weekly sermons sent to me on tape. After listening carefully to each one, I would discuss anything needing further explanation with Pastor Jeff through email. If anyone could have opened their heart and home to me via the internet, he did. I felt as though he took me under his wing and into the sanctuary. If his church had been nearby, I would've gone.

When another Vineyard church about an hour from my home planned a renewal service, I asked his advice about attending it.

He wrote back:

Remember when you go to the renewal meetings, it's like chicken. Eat the meat but spit out the bones. There will be some stuff God is doing and you are really touched by, and there will be other stuff you can't relate to or are repulsed by (usually the flesh), so don't be dismayed if you can't take it all—take in what God affirms to your heart is for you—don't be offended by what you can't understand or agree with.

I wrote him another letter:

Hi Pastor Jeff,

Thanks for the advice on the renewal service. I just finished listening to your teaching tape (Not the Righteous, but Sinners). It kind of hit home. Oh, I'm a far cry from a Pharisee (holy religious type), but rather attribute that to many Christians I know. But I can totally relate to the part about feeling as though you don't need forgiveness. Many times I feel this way, but I attribute it to the freeing of the mind process I encountered in Wicca. All Christian principles have been stripped from my mind/emotions and spirit. In a sense, I don't feel anything about it at all. It's as though I have a spiritual numbness.

Must say I thought it great when, in the teaching, you shared how Christians should be hanging out with the tax collectors of today, rather than what is normally preached about the light having nothing in common with darkness thing. It also brought a question to me about what your opinion would be regarding Matthew 18, where the church kicks out offending brethren and treats them like tax collectors?

Ally

He responded:

Glad you're being encouraged. The numbness can come from a number of sources: fear, denial, depression, even unbelief (I believe but help my unbelief). I think a lot of us are like Coke bottles when it comes to receiving God's mercy and love; we can only get a little in at a time. Given your occult involvement, you may have some unholy spirits holding you back. By the way, everyone is affected by "demons," but the more cooperation you've given them in the past, the stronger the hold they have on you; we call these strongholds. If someone prays for you in this area, don't freak out even if you find yourself freaking out. I think it would be good if you did some verbal renouncing of any "idols, voices, or channels" that you may have listened to in the past. Do this with a Christian you trust.

Re: Matt. 18, the church discipline passage. A three-step process to be used judiciously and with grace to deal with obvious sin from a person claiming to be a brother/sister in fellowship with you and your Christian community. The ultimate step (dis-fellowshipping) is really meant to be a wake-up call rather than a locked-down judgment. Look at 1 Corinthians 1:5 and 1 Corinthians 2:4–11 for more detail on this process. The underlying concept is to have a judicious way to deal with obvious (I mean obvious) sin by someone

who portrays themselves as a serious Christian. This is not
to be used when someone is coming out of a sinful pattern
but struggling to break free—it's for people who aren't struggling.

Remember, you have a lot to learn and need to give yourself time to grow. There will be some things you won't get,
won't even believe, want not to do but do anyway, want to do
but can't, etc. So keep moving ahead, but don't expect to do
it all at once.

In Him,

Jeff

Bo offered to take me to the renewal service at the Vineyard
church. After a long ride, we arrived at the old warehouse building that now served as the church. We felt at peace as soon as we
entered, and the people were warm and friendly but not over-
bearing, which was exactly what I needed. During worship, the
presence of the Lord filled the place and I experienced a sweet
comforting spirit that I had never experienced before. The Vineyard experience was a good one, and I thought it was a shame it
was so far away.

A sample worship CD was handed out to all visitors, and I
found the music very moving. Then a song came on that was totally captivating, "Spirit of the Sovereign Lord." It reminded me
of Keith Green's music and seemed familiar, though I knew I had
never heard it before. At home, I played it repeatedly as my spirit soared, and suddenly it was morning. I had spent the entire
night listening to that one song!

Bo made sure I had a continuous supply of Christian books
and articles, and encouraged me to get to as many Christian concerts as I could. One very cold night, I attended a Larry Nor-
man concert held in an old theater that didn't have a working
heater. He played well past midnight and was still playing when
I left. Never had I felt so full of hearing about Jesus without being preached to as I did that night. I saw a caring servant willing

to live his life as Jesus did, walking among sinners to tell them about the love of Jesus.

Bo recommended other concerts as well. I had to respect his great effort to make sure I was being fed while I was cast off from church. During this time, he became even more furious when I would go to a ritual. He warned me it wasn't good for me to be going without a spiritual experience in God to counter its influence. We now often fought over spiritual issues, and I found my unresolved anger at the church beginning to rise to the surface again.

Though rejected by the church, I desperately held on to the things of God through music and contact with Bo and Pastor Jeff. One cool night when all was silent and calm, I had another dream.

I was again in the outer courts of the great room, only now I could see that the room was just one in a great temple. This time the room was furnished, and many people filled it. At the front of the room, God sat on His enormous throne. Some people lay at His feet, while others danced joyfully about.

I walked outside in the corridors that surrounded the temple, among the huge stone walls and pillars. The wind blew through my hair and brushed across my face, sending my dress fluttering in the breeze. A voice told me, "Out of playfulness you have left the temple, and you wander aimlessly through my corridors being blown about by the wind."

My unresolved anger led to bitterness. My heart continued to harden toward the church and the people who called themselves Christians. I considered long and hard the reason I had reluctantly started to attend church again to answer the question, "Who do you say that I am?" At least now I could answer His question. I knew who He was, but I also discovered who I was—or, I should say, *what* I was.

I had made a choice, and nothing I could do would change what I had become. I was a witch, and no amount of church-going would make me a Christian. Gone were Christian principles and godliness, and I was no longer the same person who had committed her life to Christ so long ago. No wonder I had faced so much friction. I just couldn't seem to get over the hill. It wasn't mine to climb. Another destiny awaited me.

I sought solace at my neglected altar, lighting a white candle and burning sandalwood incense. I then scanned the room for any feline friends before letting Luna out. She cuddled beneath my chin as I stroked her orange cheek, gazing upon the image of Rhiannon. I focused on the Goddess who comforted and called her name softly. Placing my disappointments before her, I meditated on her pale horse carrying them away into the waves of the sea.

Luna began making soft melodic sounds, and her sweet song became a soothing balm for my hurting soul.

CHAPTER TWENTY

—⚭—

I focused on returning wholeheartedly to the ways of the Goddess. No longer would I exhaust energy pursuing the Christian path. I knew what path was mine—my destiny was to be her high priestess.

I arrived at the shop for the full moon ritual, robed, and took my place to anoint the conveners with oil. After sacred space was created, we each wrote our desire on a piece of parchment paper. I wrote, *Pursue my destiny as a high priestess.* We then took turns tossing our desires into the flaming cauldron.

Amber stood before the altar and invoked the Goddess. She then walked around the circle with a message for each of us. When she came to me, she looked into my eyes and said, "You already know what you are destined for." Taking a step closer, she continued, "Are you willing to make the sacrifices that are required of you?"

I stared back into her dark eyes. "I am willing."

She grabbed my hand and dropped burning wax from the candle she held into the palm of my hand. The wax burned my skin, but I didn't flinch.

"Work your magic, and you shall have your desire," she said, placing an amulet into my hand before moving on to the next person.

We closed the circle and turned the shop lights back on. Before getting in line to fill my plate for feasting, I looked at the amulet and found the symbol for high priestess.

—〜〜—

Once home, I let Cujo outside for his last call of the night. The phone rang, and I answered to a raging Bo, who exploded with anger and demanded answers. Why was I so late? I hadn't rejected God, had I? What men were there at the ritual, and how close did I get with them?

The last thing I wanted was to listen to his accusing questions, so I laid down the law: I wasn't going to answer any of his questions,

I was tired of fighting over the same issue, and if he didn't stop confronting me, I simply wouldn't speak to him when I came home from a ritual.

That didn't go over well. "What are you keeping from me?" he asked.

"Nothing. Besides, what goes on in ritual is none of your business," I snapped back.

"What happened to giving your life to God?"

"Once a witch, always a witch. My destiny is to become a high priestess."

"You're not a high priestess. You're supposed to be a prophetess of God!" Though I held the phone away from ear, I could still hear him yelling. "You don't have to stay a witch!"

With the mouthpiece in front of my lips, I screamed back, "What makes you think I would choose not to be? Not that it matters, but show me one true witch who ever became a Christian and stayed one!"

We hung up, and I decided I would no longer talk to him after ritual. At least I had a happy Cujo waiting to come back in. I headed to the dog biscuit jar with Cujo hot on my heels and awaiting a Meaty Bone. At times like these, I enjoyed the company of my dog more than I did people.

—ᘯ—

I no longer discussed spiritual things with Bo. He would remind me of Pastor John and the church's love for me, and I would turn him away by saying I knew that it was all one-sided. I no longer wanted to hear about anything he felt God was doing in his life. My mind was closed and my heart became increasingly hardened.

At the same time, Amber was ready to get back into working intense magic. (My good friend Cora was no longer with us; she had chosen to follow the Goddess religion but not one of witchcraft. I was sad to see her go, but we remained friends.) Amber started a new class for those desiring to learn the Wiccan ways, and when the course ended, she held an open circle and invited all who had completed the class. Over the next several months, more classes continued, and it wasn't long before we were working with a large group with new people and new energy.

I had been in the group the longest, so my part took on another dimension. I worked with another coven member, a short girl with shiny long black hair whose name was Autumn, as the handmaidens to our high priestess. Autumn would gather everyone together within the circle and work with them to ground (clear their minds and create a conduit for divine energy) while I assisted Amber in her preparation for ritual. An enormous amount of time and energy was put forth for full and new moon rituals. As with any large group, we had people at different levels on their path of enlightenment.

One night, Autumn and I met Amber, who closed the shop early so we could get ready for what would be an intense full moon ritual. We draped a black backdrop, blocking off a portion of the shop. Behind it we created a Goddess throne using a chair wrapped in silk material. Next to the throne we placed a table with a crystal ball and a pouch of runes on top. A Goddess tapestry Amber hand-painted hung outside the throne room.

When the others arrived, they robed and were smudged

and anointed before Amber cast the circle. We called forth the quarters, and Amber said that after she invoked the Goddess, we would each take turns meeting her. The drumming continued, and one by one I brought them to the enclosed area before returning to the circle with the others. Those of us outside the veiled area either joined in drumming, danced in place, or went into a trance while waiting for our turn. The shadows from the candle flames on the altar seemed to engage in a dance of their own.

Then I had the strange feeling that I was being watched. Opening my eyes, I saw the hand-painted tapestry of Hecate had come to life. Her eyes followed our movements; we were under surveillance.

For a moment I sat still, not wanting to draw attention to myself. Several others also stared at the tapestry, obviously witness to the eye movement. I was almost glad when the time came to escort the next person to the enclosure. Rather than return to the circle, I stood by the makeshift curtains. Intense energy permeated beyond the covering.

Then it was my turn, and I entered and found Hecate, who had been invoked by Amber and channeled through her as she sat on the throne. Her whole demeanor changed as she sat waiting for me to approach. Beneath the veil that covered her head, I saw her aged face.

"Come here," she said quietly but firmly.

Uneasiness put me on edge as I stepped forward and dropped to my knees before her.

She told me she was pleased with my devotion and then motioned for me to gaze into the crystal ball. After some time, she asked, "Tell me, what do you see?"

"I see a funnel, like a tornado blowing every which way," I said.

"That tornado is the chaos in your life. And it is destructive, if you don't put an end to its cause." She paused. "I know it's hard, but you've got to get this destructive force out of your life. Here, take this." She handed me a rune. "This is my gift that will help you succeed." She then released me, and I returned with the others.

Now that everyone had a turn, Amber came out from the veiled area and dismissed the circle.

Later, she and I discussed the need to form inner and outer circles. Amber concluded that only six people in the group would be part of the inner circle. We would meet regularly and work together, while the rest would be invited to participate in the major Sabbat rituals. The smaller group would enable deeper intimacy and focus on more intense rituals.

The six of us then gathered to discuss coven-related matters. We made official coven robes and talked about the devotion we must have to the Goddess, to one another, and to the coven. "Perfect love and perfect trust" was the motto to live by. One man who we considered to have high priest potential never returned. Amber said many more would also leave, as the ways of Wicca are not easy and not all continue down its path, but those that do find power and strength within.

Tonight would prove to be a magical night, as I was one of the few chosen to attend the Nightsong ritual led by Lady Brandilyn. After dropping my children off at their grandparents' house, I drove to The Village. Black linen hung over all the windows in the shop. We immediately robed in black, and the door was closed and locked, indicating we were about to begin ritual. Amber directed us to sit in a circle around a single black candle that now provided the only light in the room. Lady Brandilyn would cast the circle and call the quarters.

The candle was then snuffed out, leaving us in complete darkness. Anything we saw would be purely spiritual. As Lady Brandilyn called forth the quarters, I felt their presence enter in a tangible way. We sat in silence as she led us on a sacred journey, invoking the ancient Goddess and her consort. The sights, sounds, and movements we all experienced in the pitch darkness were not of this world. The language we spoke was not of this day and age, yet we understood what was being said.

The Goddess's consort shape-shifted into a leopard and prowled throughout the room. I felt a puff of air making my hair stand on end. Just then a loud thump was followed by the crash of books falling off the shelves like dominos. The leopard walked around, playfully stalking us until his golden eyes met mine. He was so close I could feel his warm breath on my face, but I didn't turn away. Rather, I focused on the eyes that looked upon me.

Soon I felt myself being drawn deeply into one of his eyes as it became a spinning kaleidoscope of many colors. I fell into the deepest part of the earth, feeling first heat and then the iciness of an eerie, rocky place that resembled a cave. Huge tree roots snaked through boulders in this place where I sat conversing with spirits of the underworld.

I was led around the bend to a rock shrine, and beneath it spread a pond as clear as a mirror. I saw the image of a very old woman wrapped in a hooded cape. When I looked up, she stood before me—the Dark Goddess robed in the depths of the night sky. Her face was the abyss.

A moment later, all that was gone and I found myself back in the circle of darkness, conversing in a language I didn't know. In what seemed too short of a time, the circle was closed and the light returned. Books lay scattered about the room, leaving evidence that we hadn't been alone.

The next day, I spoke with Amber about what I had experienced during the ritual. We talked about how everyone had seen some of the same things, yet each had their own personal experience. In complete darkness, we each saw images, colors, and shapes, and felt the movement of the Goddess's consort as he paced about the room.

"That was so great!" I said, longing for more. "Do you think

Lady Brandilyn would come back and do another?"

"I'm sure there'll be another," Amber assured me, "and you can be certain you'll be there."

—⚬—

By now my children were getting older, and I decided it was time to exchange my bus for a desk. I applied for a clerk position at a small title company and got the job. Gone were the days of waking at dawn to drive the ice-cold school bus. I was thrilled to be working in an office, and the five-hour work day enabled me to be home when the kids got out of school.

When I'd been there for about a year, I brought in a picture that had a pentacle on it to make a photocopy. One of the girls in the office asked me about it, so I came out of my broom closet and shared my beliefs.

It was a small office, and soon everyone knew. They were very open to the pagan mind-set and seemed genuinely interested in true witchcraft rather than the typical stereotypes. Before long, we had two other witches working in the office. My boss would joke that he certainly couldn't be accused of religious discrimination when it came to hiring employees.

—⚬—

Amber held open drumming circles between new and full moons. Some of us used this occasion as a way to primally connect with the earth mother, while others came simply for fun. I brought Lynn and Missy, while Aaron went to his best friend's house to play computer games. I liked the peace of mind that resulted from having the girls with me; it removed them from the emotional turmoil at home and was a fun way to introduce them to the magical realm.

A circle of drummers formed around the perimeter inside the shop. Most had brought their own djembe drums, though a drum was not required. I handed Lynn a miniature djembe and Missy a shaker, and we found a place to sit.

By now, the aroma of incense infiltrated the dimly lit room. One of our experienced drummers began a slow, steady beat, and one by one we joined in until the Spirit simply took over the rhythm and everyone was either drumming or rhythmically dancing. The beat crescendoed and suddenly stopped, leaving participants shouting, clapping, and laughing.

When we took a break, I led the girls outside for some fresh air and asked what they thought.

"It's cool but strange, Mom," Missy said.

Lynn looked down as she chewed her nails. "It's okay, I guess."

I smiled, believing it was good for them to be open to new experiences and draw their own conclusions. We then retreated inside for another round of drumming.

—m—

One of our summer full moon rituals was underway. Bo was in town, and we decided to meet for breakfast at an all-night diner after ritual. Unbeknownst to me, he had arrived early and was sitting on a bench outside a store near the shop, watching and waiting. Once ritual finished and debriefing concluded, the feasting began, so we opened the door to let in the cool midnight air. As conveners went out on the porch to get fresh air, I excused myself to meet Bo.

I said goodbye to Orion, stopping to exchange our customary embrace and kiss. As I stepped off the porch, Bo stood there looking furious. I quickly went to join him.

"Why don't you introduce me to your friend?" he said sarcastically.

"Oh, that's Orion. He's one of the coven and working on becoming our next high priest."

"Do you always kiss your high priest that way?"

"What way? Bo, get a grip!" I exclaimed. "We were just saying goodbye."

"Really? Well, I've read that some of your rituals involve sex." He grabbed my arm and looked me in the eyes. "Did you?"

"Is that all your perverted mind ever thinks about?" I pulled away and started toward the car.

He followed. "You can't say that doesn't happen. I've seen some of the books sold in that shop."

"That doesn't mean it's what I did tonight," I insisted. "It was just a kiss goodbye. Besides, what I choose to do is my business. I can't deal with your accusations."

"Then tell me about the ritual tonight. Tell me what you did."

"There are some things that can't be discussed, and magic is one of them."

When we reached the car, I stopped and put my arms around his neck. "Bo, you have nothing to worry about. I only gave my high priest a hug goodbye."

"It was more like an embrace," he said as he pulled me into his arms. "As I sat outside tonight waiting for you, I watched gays and lesbians romantically embracing one another as if it were normal. The people coming out of the bars are wasted. Sin is blatantly acted upon without remorse, and even people coming from the shop you were in seemed provocative in their demeanor."

Livid that Bo would include my coven in his observation of sin, I refused to validate his jealousy over my relationship with coven members "Don't be ridiculous."

"I heard them talking about getting laid—their words, not mine," he said, "Look around you. Don't you see there is darkness here? As I sat here tonight, I believe God showed me that this whole area is just like Sodom and Gomorrah. It's lost to sin. You know what happened to those places in the Bible, so please, you need to get away from this."

I opened my car door and quickly got in. "Then flee, Bo. Run or you might turn into a pillar of salt!"

"Don't mock God!"

I slammed my car door, then opened the window "I'm not mocking God. It's you that I have an issue with!" Then I put the car in gear and drove off.

When I looked in the rearview mirror, Bo was scrambling to follow me. I drove across the bridge and down the narrow, winding road that led out of The Village, remembering how he had once been so understanding and accepting of my beliefs. His headlights approached from behind, and I considered driving past the diner, but at the last minute I pulled into the parking lot. Hopefully he had calmed down enough that we could have a peaceful meal together.

We asked for a table in a quiet corner and, after ordering breakfast, resumed our previous conversation.

"I'm sorry if I sounded judgmental," Bo said softly. "I just don't want you to shut God out entirely."

Was he apologizing? "That's really not the issue. You've got to stop acting like I've committed some mortal crime every time I go to ritual."

"Why can't you accept that I hear from God?" he asked. "What if what I feel is right and The Village is as Sodom and Gomorrah? Don't you think it best to at least consider getting out of there?"

"I think you like to use your Christianity to control me."

"Why would I try to control you?" he asked. "That place is full of sin and idolatry and sexual perversion."

I held his gaze. "And you, Bo, are full of lust as you sit there and act like you're so holy."

"Don't compare me with that place!"

"Okay, Mr. Holy One! I dare not compare you with my life-style of perversion!" I got up to leave.

"I didn't say you!" He tried to correct himself, but I was already walking out the door

A few days passed before I talked to Bo, and we never spoke of Sodom and Gomorrah again. We just stopped talking about spiritual things and focused on music and other mutual interests. We went to several concerts but avoided the whole Christian concert scene. Bo often made visits to The Village and waited for me after ritual. I wasn't quite sure if his motive was to spy or spend time with me, but we never failed to argue after ritual. He was also threatened by my friendship with Amber and the amount of time I spent with her.

—ᴍ—

One night as the coven gathered for ritual and the Goddess was invoked, we were told that we had been chosen to help others in a time that would be coming soon. The trials, tears, and hardship we had endured were preparation for this "coming." As things concerning the approaching time were brought forth, I recognized a similarity with Scripture. It was as though I was hearing about the end times of the Bible being told in pagan terminology. Of course, the reason and outcome were not the same but the events were.

I realized that if this was indeed the end times that the Bible spoke of, I was to remain in this place to help others enduring such tribulation. From a biblical standpoint, that meant I would be one of those who were left behind and separated from the presence of God forever.

In some strange way, I accepted that as my destiny.

CHAPTER TWENTY-ONE

—⟋⟍—

As summer came to an end, news headlines touted the effects of global warming on the nation. Remembering what we had heard at ritual, I sat down at my computer to reflect on the latest reports. Suddenly I was in the midst of another vision.

Breaking News: Scientists Discover a Link between Current Catastrophes and Global Warming. The image of the blood-red moon hit the television screen and then the station displayed the devastation of the recent earthquake in New York City. This was not global warming, and I called my children into the room to tell them what was happening.

"Mom, chill," was their response. "It's only an increase in the earth's temperature!"

"No!" I proceeded to tell them about the events in the book of Revelation, then insisted that we pray. The next thing I knew, we were at the foot of a mountain and Michael was with us. We knew we had to go there, as did the other people who were all around. As we climbed the mountain, we came to a camp that Pastor John and my former church family occupied.

"I see you made it!" someone said.

"Yeah," I replied.

In my heart, I sensed that these were God's people but there was something about them that displeased the heart of God. I told the children and Michael that we needed to keep moving. We came across another camp of people, and I heard God say that they were His children too, but again something displeased Him and we needed to keep going.

This continued through seven camps.

When we reached the top of the mountain, the clouds opened and an enormous white horse descended from the heavens. I knew Jesus was on that horse. Turning, I looked down the mountain to where a multitude of people watched in awe. My church family stood near the foot of the mountain, and suddenly I understood. A voice said, "The last shall be first!" and I fell to my knees in worship. It finally all came together.

—◊◊◊—

I arrived home from work one rainy day and found a letter from Pastor John. *Perhaps it's a letter of apology?* I thought as I tore open the envelope. Inside was a letter and the bulletin from my wedding. The letter read:

> I ran across the enclosed while cleaning my basement files. Thought you might remember the good times, just for old time's sake. You and Michael were the first couple I married. Might be a coincidence, but every couple I married who stayed in New Zion is still married.
>
> May the Lord bless you in your search for happiness. Some say they could only find true and lasting peace and joy in Jesus.
>
> My Love to All,
>
> John

I was appalled. Why would he send something so sentimental back to me? Was he ending my presence in his life, or was he just trying one last ditch effort to draw me back? I didn't know how to respond. I took a few weeks to think it over before responding.

Dear John,

Thank you for sending me the wedding bulletin you found in your basement. I know we were the first couple you married, and I've often felt as though I've let you down. If so, I'm sorry. I appreciate all your efforts in trying to make it work.

It's kind of hard to reminisce about the "good ole days" when you are the recipient of another's unwillingness to keep such memories going.

A few weeks ago, I was looking through our wedding photo album with my girls. I had a husband, spiritual family/friends that I guess I took for granted, thinking their love would always be there. I realized, as a Keith Green song goes, that nothing lasts except for the grace of God.

This began a brief email correspondence between us as we shared our own interpretation of the church's response to my witchcraft involvement. I felt a whole kaleidoscope of emotions as I read Pastor John's emails, but one sentence infuriated me:

Your moral debt was canceled, being stamped PAID in bright red blood—blood you didn't shed; blood that says I love you, Ally; blood that no Isis, or other demon-created godlette can stand because it echoes in time and eternity to say, "I LOVE YOU!"

As I reread every word, rage burned within me. How dare he call the Goddess a demon or a created godlette! What angered me most was that I still felt the need to gain Pastor John's approval. It was time to end this pseudo-father-figure relationship once and for all.

The night was pre-arranged, but it seemed to be perfect timing for cutting the apron strings from Pastor John's fatherly influence. Amber had scheduled the banishing ritual to get rid of negative influences in our lives before I knew I even needed it. The negative influence in my life was Pastor John, and it was way past time to let go and allow those wounds to heal.

We gathered on the night of the dark moon and robed ourselves in black. The cauldron and a black candle sat on top of the
altar. In the candlelight, we cast our circle and called quarters.
Amber announced our intent to banish all negative influences,
and with this focus in mind, the drumming intensified as the
energy rose within the circle. Amber then invoked Hecate and lit
the banishing candle. I focused on Pastor John and his negative
influence. I envisioned him far away from having any impact on
me. Adrenaline rushed through me as I dwelled on my hurt and
rejection.

The drumming grew louder and faster along with my anger.
I approached the altar and took the small piece of envelope con-
taining Pastor John's return address and held it tightly between
my fingers. I focused on him calling the Goddess a demon and
godlette. When I felt as though the energy within was about to
burst, I set the paper on fire using the banishing candle's flame.
I envisioned the negative influence being lifted from me, then
stepped away from the altar to allow the next covener to do their
banishing.

When all had finished, we joined together and released the
energies into the universe to do our bidding. Amid a climatic
drum beat and shout, the final annunciation, "So mote it be,"
was made and the circle was closed.

—⚹—

Not long afterward, Bo called to ask me to speak with a woman who ran a ministry for those desiring to get out of the Craft.
He told me she had been a Wiccan high priestess and would like
to talk to me.

"If a former Wiccan high priestess wants to pursue the Christian path, that's fine," I told him, "but what's that got to do with
me?"

"You said there was no one around who ever made it out, and
she has," he pointed out.

I considered that. "Anyone who leaves the Wiccan path always returns sooner or later."

"Not this woman. She's been out for ten years now," he said. "Will you at least talk to her?"

I sighed. "Actually, I just got this letter from Pastor John calling the Goddess a demon. I have zero tolerance for Christians right now."

"But she was once where you are today, and I don't think she'll call your Goddess a demon. I told her about the church and all. She agrees they are in the wrong."

"That's because it is wrong!"

"Just talk with her, okay?" he suggested. "Nobody is asking you to change your beliefs. Just talk with her. Please?"

"Okay. I guess I can do that much."

So now Bo was setting up a phone conversation with an ex-Wiccan. What next? How many avenues would this man try? It didn't really bother me to speak with her, as I was tried and true to my path. Besides, there was nothing she could tell me that I didn't already know. In a sense, this conversation seemed meaningless. I grew skeptical, wondering if she would be yet another overzealous Christian ready to save the world from evil or an ex-witch wannabe now performing to gullible Christian audiences.

The conversation was nothing of the sort. I spoke with Rosa, who was soft-spoken, kind, and knew the Craft. We talked mostly about the church and the misunderstandings they had with Wiccans, along with their well-meaning attempts to save souls with their fire-and-brimstone approach and my own shunning from the church family. She understood where I was coming from, as well as the church's well-meaning but unwarranted treatment of someone like me.

After we spoke for about a half an hour, Rosa ended the conversation with a warm, "Blessed be ... in Jesus." She used a common Wiccan goodbye but added *in Jesus*, which boggled my mind.

—⚹—

I soon received an email from Pastor Jeff, my long-distance pastor. He included a link to his church's website, which included a picture of him and a brief description of the journey that led him to be senior pastor. To my surprise, he looked like a mature radical from the Jesus Freak movement, not the typical prim and proper pastor with a Bible in hand. I read about his family and all the different church functions taking place at the Vineyard.

Afterward, I emailed him back saying that I thought the church website was cool and that it was interesting to see the person I had been writing to. I also told him about my own website, which included a picture of me, but I warned him he probably wouldn't want to see it since I was dressed in ritual garb and had an animated Luna flying across my page dedicated to the Goddess. He responded that he would still like the link to the website if I was willing to share it and would keep my pagan mind-set in consideration.

A good week passed before Pastor Jeff replied, saying he had indeed checked out my website. He hadn't realized the extent of my involvement until he saw it on the screen—a priestess with poetry and invocations to the Goddess, not a searching soul caught between two belief systems as he had expected. As I read his response, a sense of alarm rose within me. Would he be like the others and turn me away? As if anticipating my concern, he reassured me that nothing had changed and he wasn't going to stop writing to me.

As I breathed a sigh of relief that I wouldn't have to endure yet another shunning, I read his closing words to me: "You cannot serve both God and Rhiannon (mammon)."

I would have expected such a remark coming from Pastor John, but Pastor Jeff? He had such a gentle spirit about him and had always been kind, caring, and quick to extend grace. That remark just didn't seem to fit his character. The more I thought about it, the funnier it seemed. Suddenly, I couldn't help but laugh.

—◊—

The moon had waxed and waned since the banishing ritual, so I sent a short email to Pastor John to see if it had worked. Not expecting an answer, I was surprised when he replied. He explained he was retiring as senior pastor, their house was for sale, and they would be moving out of the state.

I stared at the screen in disbelief. What had I done? Did his move have anything to do with my banishing spell? I remembered the day when he had predicted that I would one day work magic against those I loved. At the time, I thought it ridiculous; after all, magic was always used for the good of all and never in a negative way. I hadn't believed him, but here I sat contemplating the repercussions of what I'd done.

How could I consider removing him from my life as something positive? I got what I wanted, but was it what I really needed? A deep sense of loss and sorrow came over me. He was a servant of Jesus, and surely other realms had no power over those covered in the blood. Still, I felt I had to level with Pastor John before he went ahead with such a drastic step. I called him.

"Well, hello there, my gal!" he said. "It's been a while since I've heard from you."

"Yes, it has." I tried to figure out how to tell him what was on my mind. "I just got your email. What's this about retiring and moving? Where are you moving to?"

"Well, we're not really sure, but it looks like we'll be moving down South."

I took a deep breath. "I need to tell you something that may have some bearing on that decision. I can only hope you'll find it within yourself to forgive me."

His tone became more serious. "What would make you question my forgiving you?"

"Well, there's the shunning and list of requirements to come back to church, to name a few. But honestly, it's not why I'm calling. I've done something I never thought I would." Once the words started, they just poured out like a flood. "It's just that I felt guilty for not meeting your expectations."

"Well, I'm not sure that's a bad thing." He now sounded a bit confused.

"No, but I got to a point that I was really angry about it. Angry with myself, really, because I couldn't let go, and so I took things in my own hands. Well, not really my own hands. Anyway, I did a banishing."

"What's a banishing?"

"I cut the ties to you. I felt I had to remove your influence from my life."

"You cast a spell against me, your good old friend John?" he asked, obviously hurt. "How could you?"

"It was out of hurt and not being able to just let go," I cried. "I'm sorry just doesn't say enough."

The conversation was short, as I really couldn't explain how bad I felt. When we hung up, I wondered if he would ever find it within his heart to truly forgive me. He took spells and that sort of thing as a work of the enemy, and what I'd done wouldn't be something easily overlooked. It made me think about my state of mind, and examine the depths I would go for the sake of what I felt was a hindrance to me.

A few weeks later, Pastor John emailed me. His note was short and to the point. A woman who had previously been involved in the occult but was now a Christian had started attending New Zion. He thought it might be a good idea for me to talk with her and was extending an open invitation—what he called a "heaven-for-a-day pass"—for me to come to church so I could meet her.

I didn't know how to respond after being shunned three times and vowing never to walk through those doors again. Honestly, I wanted to go just for spite and to prove that I could walk through those doors and nothing could stop me. I had no desire for the things of God, and had long since dismissed the sense of family I thought I once had at that church.

I couldn't help wondering about this woman. She could have been a Satanist for all they knew. The church considered us all one and the same, whether we only read horoscopes, practiced Wicca, or worshiped Satan. I finally decided to take him up on the offer, if only for spite. I could easily say hello to this woman, let her speak her mind, and quickly dismiss myself, end of story.

Pastor John told me he would let the elders know I'd be attending church next Sunday, then informed me he would be out of town and would have Pastor Jacob oversee our conversation. I felt like I was being thrown to a pack of hungry wolves, knowing the elders wouldn't be thrilled to have a witch among them.

I wasn't looking forward to the meeting but determined not to let anything stop me. I told him I'd be there.

When I woke up early on Sunday morning, Michael was already on the computer and the kids were sleeping in after a late-night movie marathon. They had reached the stage of claiming their own independence, so following Mom was now considered uncool. That was just as well since I would likely be late getting home since I'd be meeting with the woman who claimed to be an ex-witch.

I arrived at the church a few minutes early and made my way to the last seat against the far wall. I couldn't help but be a little nervous and uncomfortable. People weren't overly friendly, but they weren't hostile either, and a few of the old-timers even greeted me. Within a few minutes, I had composed myself and become more relaxed.

The service opened with a prayer and then we stood for worship. Everything appeared the same and yet something was different, though I couldn't put my finger on it. Suddenly, tears streamed from my eyes and down my cheeks. I had no idea why I was crying; I wasn't upset about anything, but I couldn't hold them back. The whole experience confused me, and by the time the music ended I felt exhausted. I sat down, relieved to hear there would be a baby dedication this morning. At least that would be lighthearted; I felt like I'd been hit by a Mack truck.

I leaned against the wall and pulled my cape around me like a child holding on to a security blanket. Every ounce of energy had seemingly been drained from my body. After the baby dedication, the children were dismissed and the teaching began. Without warning, I began crying again. I didn't even know what was being taught, but just being there had a major impact on me. I cried through the whole service and couldn't wait to leave.

On my way out, one of the home group leaders let me know that the woman I was supposed to meet wasn't there. That was fine with me. I just wanted to get out of there!

I cried for three days before I finally called Pastor John. "You know I went to church Sunday," I began.

"Yeah, how'd it go?" he asked.

"Actually, that's why I called. I've been crying for three days straight, and I don't know why. It started during worship, and I cried though the whole service even though I'm not upset about anything. This is so confusing."

"Honey, you're just being touched by God," he said in his fatherly voice.

"I've been touched by God before, but this is different. I can't stop crying, and there is no reason to cry. I felt so drained in church. Why?"

"Well, God knows exactly what we need," he said, "so if He touched you in a way you aren't used to, it's because it's what you need right now with where you are."

I wasn't convinced. "So this is just me being touched by God? Oh, and I never got to meet that woman you talked about."

"I heard she wasn't there. Sorry about that."

"Well, can I maybe get another get-into-heaven-for-a-day pass and come back another time when she'll be there?" I didn't so much want to meet with this woman, but see if I encountered the same experience as I had the week before. That would prove it was just an isolated incident.

"Yeah, no problem," Pastor John said. "I'll speak with the elders about you coming back this Sunday. I'm sure she'll be there this week. I won't be there again since I'm leaving on Thursday, but I'll arrange for you to go before I leave."

The next day, I received a confirmation from Pastor John saying all was arranged for my coming to church again on Sunday. Then it hit me that this Sunday was Samhain. I would be up all night at the traditional Witches' Ball for ritual and feasting, so I wouldn't be getting home until the early morning hours and the last place I would want to go would be church. I thought about asking for a different day but didn't think they'd warrant my coming home from ritual late as a good excuse.

For now, I would just focus on the upcoming Sabbat and see how the rest of it fell into place.

A WITCH'S ENCOUNTER WITH GOD

CHAPTER TWENTY-TWO

—⁂—

D id I really want to get out of my nice comfy bed and go to church after only two hours of sleep? After all, it had been well after four a.m. by the time I got to bed after the Samhain ritual, and sleeping in like most other pagans seemed the way to go. Besides, after being charged with energy the night before, I couldn't expect that I'd experience anything at church, even if it was in the supernatural.

I arrived just before the service began, so I had to sit in the middle of the church but still managed to get a seat in the back row. The service began almost immediately, and as everyone stood for worship, I found myself crying uncontrollably once again. I was beside myself, especially after where I had been the night before. Overwhelmed, I felt like I had to get out of there or I'd burst.

Just as I grabbed my belongings to make a swift exit, a woman of African descent approached me. I didn't know her, but she put her arms around me and held me as she whispered, "God just wants you to know that He loves you."

With that, I cried harder, though I was certain she hadn't the faintest idea what she was talking about. Surely God didn't love me, not after all I had done. *Christians always say that to visitors,* I thought to myself. She didn't know she was saying it to someone who had walked away from the faith and into witchcraft. I convinced myself that if she knew I was a witch, she wouldn't be saying that.

Worship ended, so I sat down with everyone else, not wanting to draw attention to myself by leaving. Pastor Lyndon announced that the teaching would concern the biblical perspective of the well-marketed holiday known as Halloween. I should have known this would be the subject taught in Christian churches today.

Well, there was no way I was going to sit there and listen to my beliefs being ridiculed and torn to pieces by their rhetoric. But before I could leave, the same woman who had hugged me sat down beside me and took me by the hand. She whispered, "You're going to think this crazy, but God told me I was supposed to come sit beside you and hold your hand."

Now what was I supposed to do? I didn't want to be rude to this stranger who was making every effort to be nice to me. So I sat there, becoming more and more furious about the things being said. How dare he make such accusations when he had no idea what he was talking about! He could have at least gotten the pronunciation correct. There were times I had to bite my tongue not to interrupt and speak the truth of the matter. When the teaching ended, the woman beside me returned to her seat.

As Pastor Lyndon announced that we were going to pray against the enemy as the Lord led, I gathered my belongings and stood to leave. Katie, one of the home group leaders, intercepted and introduced me to Tina, the woman I had come to meet. I politely said hello but looked longingly at the door. I'd had enough for the day—and enough for a long time, really.

"Let's sit and talk," Tina suggested as Katie sat beside me.

Tina shared how she had been into Satanism. I had suspected as much. She seemed to feel there was some connection in the spiritual realm. I just wanted her to finish her story and say a prayer for me so I could get out of there. She then asked if I worshiped Satan.

"No!" I exclaimed.

"Satan is the god of the witches," she explained. "He is disguised in the Goddess you worship."

I was only halfheartedly listening to her, but her accusation caught my attention. "No, Satan and the Goddess are not one and the same." I fidgeted in my chair, anticipating her big finish.

"What is your Craft name?" she asked.

"If you were a witch, you'd know better than to ask that," I pointed out. She had to be crazy if she thought I would tell her that.

"Were you part of a coven?"

"Yes, I'm part of a coven," I confirmed.

Tina wouldn't settle for just that. She wanted to know what coven, but I wasn't about to tell her. She then asked another taboo question: "Are you initiated, and if so, what level?"

I twirled my hair between my fingers, annoyed with her intrusion. "I'm initiated, and you should know I'm not going to tell you what degree."

Tina pushed for answers, and I resisted. She asked if she could pray for me, which I quickly agreed to, relieved it was finally over so I could be on my way. Then she started casting out demons and had the nerve to include witchcraft in that category. I'd had enough and looked for a way to exit.

The service had ended and the place was almost empty. The chairs had been stacked away, and the room had been reset for the nursery school that was held there during the week. I was surrounded by a section of bookshelves, and there was only one way out, but Pastor Lyndon, Katie, and her husband, Keith, stood blocking the opening. I had no idea how I ended up enclosed in an area with these prayer warriors, but I wanted out. I stood up and thanked Tina for the prayers, then politely told her I needed to get going. She laid her hands on my head and prayed even more. The others placed their hands on me and joined in with intensity.

Tina began denouncing spiritual influences in my life, and when I actually felt as though energy was leaving my body, I decided this had to stop. I pushed Tina's hands down and shouted,

"Stop! I've had enough."

Undaunted, she laid her hands back on my head, and they all began praying even more fervently. I broke free from her hold, then ducked beneath Keith's arms and dashed out the door.

Once outside, I took a deep breath and tried to calm myself, relieved that they hadn't followed me. Then I realized I'd left my purse behind, which of course included my car keys. Here I was, stranded in the church parking lot. I stood there for a few minutes, trying to figure out what to do next, when I saw three women going into the church. I had my solution.

"I left my purse and shawl inside," I told them. "Would you be so kind and bring them out?" I figured the good Christian women would certainly honor my unusual request.

They looked a little puzzled but agreed.

Five minutes later, they returned smiling but without my purse and shawl. One of them said, "Have a nice day," as they got in their car. I knew the others must still be inside waiting for me to come back in and were using my purse as bait.

I considered my options. It was a long walk home, but I had nothing else to do, and considering the alternative, that might not be a bad idea. I could call Amber to come and get me, but how would I explain my being in a church parking lot with my purse still inside with these crazed Christians? I opened the door and walked back inside, knowing sooner or later I would have to face them. They stood conversing near the same cubicle of bookshelves, still praying. I quickly gathered my purse and shawl, all the while keeping an eye on the exit.

As I turned to leave, Pastor Lyndon said in a gentle voice, "You can't run from God."

I stopped dead in my tracks and just stood there.

"God loves you, and He is never going to stop pursing you," he went on.

The praying in tongues stopped and everyone was silent.

Pastor Lyndon continued to share. "Neither you, nor I, nor any demonic influence or anything else for that matter, will ever separate you from God's love. No matter what you may believe yourself to be, you were a Christian first and nothing you can ever do will change that."

We sat on a couple of the chairs outside the enclosed area and talked. I shared my crying spree the week before and about what I was feeling that very day.

He said, "No matter how far you run from God, He will never stop loving you. It's just a matter of how long will you keep running?"

I didn't know what hit me. It felt as though a giant waterfall had burst with me beneath it and an unexplainable love flowed over me. In that instant, the scales fell from my eyes and all the rejection, hurt, and control I had suffered at the hands of religion and men were insignificant in comparison to God's all-consuming presence. I sat speechless as my eyes grew watery, defenseless as the fortress around my heart gave way. My soul lay bare and vulnerable before Him.

My heart pounded so hard that I could hear it pulsating. And then God supernaturally swept me up. Nothing else mattered as I encountered Him with a passion so fierce that it was as if He was a relentless lion and I, His wandering offspring. His presence was menacing, and I felt faint, embraced by His indescribable strength. I had come with a malicious intent to dismiss this stirring in my soul, only to be awestruck by the power of His indescribable love.

"Ally, all you have to do is turn back to Jesus," Pastor Lyndon said. "Do you want me to pray with you now?"

How could I say no to God's love? I felt like a dark cloud had burst and the floodgates of heaven rained down on me as I bent over, bowed my head, and prayed, "Jesus, forgive me for the wrong I've done." Mascara ran down my cheeks, and I could taste salt on my lips as I recited the words Pastor Lyndon spoke: "Jesus, I surrender my life back into your hands and invite you to rule and reign in my heart from this day forward."

This time when I walked out of church, it was with an out-pouring of their love and affection as they each embraced me before I left. I drove home, trying to make sense of it all. Never in a million years would I have thought this would happen, especially on this day and in this church. There was still so much I didn't understand, but for now I was on a honeymoon in total bliss.

At home, I met Aaron walking up to the porch steps.

"Lynn's been looking for you," he said as he held the door and I walked inside.

Lynn came running down the stairs. "Were you at church this whole time?" she asked.

"Church was over long ago. We were sitting around talking," I explained.

She ran back upstairs, obviously satisfied with my answer.

Unable to contain myself any longer, I called Bo, knowing he would want to hear about my encounter.

He immediately put up his usual defense. "Don't let them get you down. There are plenty of other churches you can go to."

"For once, shut up and listen," I interrupted. "This is far greater than you could possibly imagine." My startling news then rendered him speechless.

I awoke early the next morning, still feeling God's loving presence surrounding me. The phone rang, and I was pleased to hear Pastor John's voice on the line. He told me he had received a call from Pastor Lyndon and wanted to talk to me about what God had done. Unlike during our past calls, I was no longer on the defensive and the conversation wasn't stressed. It was like talking to him again for the first time.

He said he and Joan would be home in a few weeks and he would see me then. I could hardly wait for their return.

—◊—

The following Sunday, I went to church without a get-into-heaven-for-a-day pass. This time I was embraced in their midst. Tears streamed again as I began to worship, and I felt as though I was being cleansed, though I really didn't understand from what. There were no words to express the magnitude of all I experienced that first Sunday back.

When the service ended, I approached Pastor Jacob and Liz, as all the bad feelings I had toward them had simply vanished. I eagerly told them how God, in His infinite power, had come to rescue and restore me. It was beyond my understanding how He could still love me, but after receiving His love, I could do nothing but love in return.

A few weeks later, I walked into church and to my surprise saw Pastor John and Joan. She immediately pulled me into a comforting embrace. We hugged, teary-eyed at the wonders of God's love and of my homecoming. The gap that had held my spiritual parents and friends at such a distance seemed to have disappeared, and I found myself in the arms of total acceptance. I turned around to see Pastor John standing there smiling, waiting to hug me as well. It was good to be home at last.

Ironically, I was finally back inside the church doors, but the one person who had been there through it all, Pastor John, was retiring. Pastor Lyndon would step into his place as senior pastor. Like a child who assumed her parents would remain the same and always be there, I had returned home to find my spiritual dad was not only leaving his position at the church but also moving to a different state. This seemed so unfair, but at the same time I remembered the spell I had done, and the feeling of being somewhat responsible weighed heavily on my mind.

Pastor John reassured me that everything was in God's timing, and began placing me under Pastor Lyndon's spiritual authority. He told me to stay close to Pastor Lyndon and gently guided me in that direction if I had a question or wanted prayer.

My old friend abandonment returned, only to be tossed aside with the knowledge that John was looking out for my best interest. It wouldn't be long before he would no longer be here, and I needed to have a good rapport with Pastor Lyndon when that day arrived.

One would think that after experiencing such supernatural encounters with God, I would have immediately turned from my pagan ways, but it wasn't that easy. Getting into worship was difficult, especially when the words to one song spoke about deep crying out to deep, which was also a pagan chant to the goddess Inanna. I stopped singing and had to regroup on where I was.

As I attempted to get back into worship, I looked up and locked eyes with Pastor Lyndon. I felt like I was under observation for my "praise" performance and became uneasy as I saw my spiritual worlds collide.

When the service ended, Joan approached me with a large gift bag. "A friend gave this to me in England, and I thought it would suit you." I opened the bag to find a beautifully woven gray cape. "I thought it would be a more appropriate color," she said.

I put the cape on and it fit perfectly.

"Don't you want to throw the old one away?"

I liked the cape, but saw no reason for discarding my old one. "Thank you, Joan. I'll wear the gray and put the black one in the bag to take home." I walked outside, and a gust of air almost blew the cape right off my shoulders. I grabbed it and pulled it even tighter as the east wind made its presence known.

At home, I got out of the car and glanced up to see the Mourning Moon on the horizon. With it came temptation. I hurried toward the house, staring down at the walkway as if not looking at the moon would ward off my desire.

Inside, I slammed the door closed behind me and took a deep breath. How would I resist the urge when magic was all around me? And then I wondered, *What's so wrong with the magic of creation? After all, hasn't God created it all?* I seized the opportunity and halfheartedly prayed, "Lord Jesus, break my heart of the things that break yours."

"Mom!" Lynn came running down stairs.

"What's up?" I asked, meeting her at the bottom step.

"Can I borrow the car? I need to get some mascara."

Where had the time gone? My little girl was now asking for car keys and makeup. "Sure, Lynn. Just be careful and don't lose the keys."

"Ya think?" Lynn grabbed the keys when I'd barely lifted them out of my purse, then headed out.

To my amazement, Pastor Lyndon extended grace to me and embraced me with love without restrictions. When the next full moon approached, it became tremendously hard to resist the temptation of ritual. Everything inside of me seemed to blend with the ebb and flow of the moon. He simply said he trusted God to speak to me in His timing— an acceptance that was new to me. I'd had an argument already prepared, but no defense was needed. Instead, I was offered grace in such a loving way that I didn't know how to respond.

—m—

In my mind's eye, I saw a vagabond hitchhiking in the desert with a sign that read *Egypt*. The lyrics "Why'd He get so mad about that golden cow?" from Keith Green's "So You Wanna Go Back to Egypt," a song about the Israelites desiring to return to Egypt, came to mind.

Amber, puzzled by the smirk I didn't know I had on my face, demanded, "What?"

"Oh ... nothing," I stammered. "I was just thinking of Egypt."

"I've been getting a lot on my past life recently and decided to work Egyptian magic tonight."

At hearing a knock on the door, I opened it to the others

who'd arrived for ritual. They robed, and I took my place within the circle. Amber addressed the afterlife, but my thoughts were on eternal life; the feather of Ma'at had no weight on that! (Ma'at was the goddess of truth, and the feather was balanced against the dead soul's heart to determine their fate.) Amber then stood before the altar and invoked Ma'at. She turned around, feather in hand, and proceeded to walk about the circle, prophesying what was needed to restore balance in our lives before placing an Egyptian oracle card in our hand. The circle was closed in the usual way, then we ate and debriefed. I hurried out as quickly as I could.

After ritual, I went to meet with ex-witch Rosa and her husband, Will, who had driven from Massachusetts. It was the first time I would actually meet those from Set Free Ministries. Rosa was a soft-spoken petite woman of Mexican descent with beautiful long black hair. Will was tall and thin with curly light brown hair, and he spoke in an articulate manner. We spent several hours conversing in their hotel room, with Rosa sharing in detail her journey to Wicca as well as her walk out of it. We seemed to have a common bond. Not a "cape-flapper" or dabbler, she had been a true witch and knew what I was talking about. We had both experienced a level of intimacy in a coven that we hadn't experienced at church.

Although others expected an instant conversion, she spoke of the walk as a process that takes time, as obstacles that Christians sometimes misunderstand must be overcome. Rosa also shared her journals so I could see the struggles she'd encountered along the way. She told me the church had sometimes been callous to her not fully understanding the immensity of the battle. I agreed wholeheartedly since I had experienced the same thing.

The next day, we drove to a park near The Village and spent the day walking along the river. We took a tour through a historical building where a president once slept. The cat playfully rolling around in the herb garden and the smell of maple wood burning in the fireplace provoked thoughts of another time, but I quickly dispelled them.

As we walked through the woods, Will looked for the perfect branch for a shepherd's staff, and we talked about our lives and our families, but mostly about the things of God. They spoke of the ministry that God had called them to—helping people walk out of the occult and into the light of Jesus. We then had a late lunch at a tiny restaurant overlooking the river and enjoyed a wonderful time of fellowship. A sisterhood that I desperately needed was beginning to emerge.

The next morning, they came to church with me before heading home. The time for them to go had come all too soon, but they reassured me they would be praying for me. As they got into their car, Rosa turned and said with a smile, "Blessed be in Jesus."

In the months that followed, I became aware of how much things around me had changed. It seemed I had been caught up in a fantasy land in which things appeared unchanged, or perhaps I had wandered into the land of the fairies where it is said the enchantment keeps one from experiencing time as we know it. Even driving down the street brought a new awareness as I noticed old buildings had been torn down or new neighborhoods had emerged. It was like having moved away from home and returning years later to find the neighborhood totally reconstructed. I emailed Pastor Lyndon concerning the changes underway:

Hi Lyndon,

Remember when I was over at your house talking with you and Bethany, when you mentioned getting John and Joan to pray and fast with you for the situation with Michael? Well, I would really like to do that because it's becoming desperate. Guess I hadn't realized my emotional state, kind of like being in a place where your continued existence seems determined by the instinct of survival. This time I decided to try hard to keep from taking things in my own hands and instead attempt the inevitable by trusting my circumstances, my life to God. Easier said than done, but I don't want to continue in the same mistake.

Well, the phone was shut off (Michael not paying the bill), which placed me out of touch both by phone and email. I missed church and prayer meeting, not wanting to leave my kids without a means to contact me in case of trouble with their dad. Staying home in this environment is not good. In fact, it's almost unbearable when I have to go to work and be in a constant panic wondering if things will be okay at home. Needless to say, the financial situation is an ongoing fiasco. I remember your saying something in regard to asking God to do something drastic and watch what He will do. Well, I'm ready to ask. My cry to Him has been to either bring Michael to complete wholeness and healing, to give him both the capability and desire to truly be a husband and father, or to dissolve this in a friendly manner in the best interest of the children and to provide for our means. Is that okay to ask of Him?

While driving home the other day, I was thinking how I regret all the time I wasted running everywhere except under the spiritual counsel of my spiritual parents (John and Joan). I could have learned so much from them, and they could have imparted so much of God to me that I would be in a better place today. For the first time, I really can say I regret the choice I made. I've shed a lot of tears, but this goes deeper. I realized what I regret all the more is my walking away from my heavenly Father ... all those wasted years. For the first time, I feel sorry for having done that. But then, isn't that what I was praying for when I asked, "Break my heart of the things that break yours?"

I realize how fragile this is. This is just a crack in the door; there are many more things behind it. I must deal with the years I chose to wander in the wilderness. I know God can forgive me, but can I forgive myself?

Another first, I began thinking in terms of my children's

spiritual well-being. I know this may seem strange; others have expressed concern to pray for them, but I didn't see the urgency. I have begun to realize their state with God and how what I have done has affected them in their own beliefs.

Lastly, I'm feeling abandoned again. Kind of strange because so many years ago I walked away from God in desperation, feeling abandoned by Him. Here I am, in the same circumstances, only this time I *know* my Father in heaven has not left me, for His abundant love surrounds me, but I am still dealing with this. The prodigal son (daughter) comes home, his father runs to greet him, says welcome home and by the way I'm leaving for Judea! What's wrong with that picture? I know that parable has a higher significance than that of an earthly father. I know God is pleased with my return, but that doesn't make it any easier to deal with my spiritual dad's leaving. I know, if anyone, you can understand this. The invitations for your setting-in are out. I really want to witness your setting-in, but to witness John's sending off would be too much for me to deal with.

Blessings, Ally

The TV screen took center stage with a video collage of church overseers sharing their hearts. The mood became bittersweet when Pastor John stood at the podium to preach his last sermon as senior pastor, but my thoughts were on what would've happened if I hadn't come back to see this day. I would have been devastated, having called him only to hear the voice of a stranger answering the phone. Though thankful it hadn't come to that, I still struggled emotionally with his retirement.

Over the last few months, Pastor John had gently moved me from under his counsel to under Pastor Lyndon's. It had been a difficult transition for me, especially since I still felt guilty for his leaving, but it also gave me a sense of assurance and rapport with Pastor Lyndon. I knew I was headed for a difficult day if I chose to return later in the evening for the setting-in ceremony. I really couldn't bear the thought of going, but just the same, how could I not?

That evening, I walked into church and found my way upstairs to the sanctuary. Pastor Timothy's wife, Rachel, motioned for me to sit with her and a few other women. She was a bit younger than I, outgoing and friendly and always reaching out to those around her. She had come to the church during the time I was away, but I remembered Pastor Timothy had been one of the deacons.

The church was crowded with familiar faces, as some who had left the church over the years had returned to witness this event. Quite a few pastors from different churches were there as well. The service began with a joyful celebration of worship, then the elders and pastors gathered around, sending John off into his new season of ministry.

I sat in the church pew and cried, as did many others, only my tears were not of joy but sorrow. All those years I had become convinced that when Pastor John spoke, it was the absolute truth, as if it was coming from God Himself. Now I was grieving the years lost because of my shunning. After the prayers for Pastor John ended, the time arrived for Pastor Lyndon's setting-in. The service took on more of a celebratory tone as it drew to an end, but not my tears.

Rachel directed me to Pastor John, who was standing at the front of the church sharing with the other pastors. I was reluctant to go, but she insisted it was something I needed to do.

As I tried to gain my composure, Joan turned to see me approaching and took me in her arms and said, "God is in this, as hard as it may seem. We only need to trust that He will take care of us all." She then escorted me to Pastor John, who smiled and gave me a big hug as I started to sob.

Left speechless, he put his hands on my shoulders and moved me toward Pastor Lyndon, whose awaiting hands replaced Pastor John's.

"Ally, I know how hard it was for you to come tonight, but it's good that you did," Pastor Lyndon said.

I couldn't bring myself to go to their reception, and as I made my way to my car, I cried even harder. Driving away, I realized that just as I was grieving for the time lost under Pastor John and Joan's counsel, my heavenly Father had grieved for that lost time with me. Suddenly, the prayer I had prayed, "Break my heart of the things that break yours," came alive. How much God's heart must have broken during the time I had wandered so far away from Him!

Now I was experiencing that same heartbreak.

Pastor John and Joan's house sold quickly. In many ways, their home had been the church building for a lot of us. Countless prayer meetings and counseling sessions had taken place in the living room.

Plans were made for their move, with dates set for those in the church who wanted to help. I had been laid off from work, so I had plenty of time available, but I wrestled with whether I could handle it. I remembered how they had helped me and others so many times by packing boxes, cleaning cabinets, and making beds. Even though helping them pack would be just as difficult as attending the setting-in service, this was something I needed to do. I called and let Pastor John know I was on my way.

When I arrived, the house was full of ladies from church busily packing boxes. Joan greeted me with a hug and told me she had just packed a little Precious Moments figurine snow globe I had given her years before. The figurine was a childlike woman holding a string of hearts with an inscription that so fit Joan: "You have touched so many hearts." She sent me to Pastor John, who was in a small room in the basement sorting through boxes of his teaching tapes.

He asked me to sort them, arrange them in chronological order, and file them in specially designed cases. As I began putting them in piles according to year, I realized each tape represented a Sunday I wasn't in church and how much time had gone by.

God met me right there in the basement. As I arranged the tapes, He was rearranging my heart. When I finally finished, Joan called me into the family room to show me a video her daughter had made for her birthday the year before. The video was a "this is your life" kind of montage set to the Amy Grant song "Oh, How the Years Go By." Photos from Joan's youth right up to the present day filled the screen.

I wasn't in any of them. Some of the photos were of a church group that went to Israel. Pastor John had invited me along, thinking that seeing the place where Jesus once walked the earth might help my unbelief. I had declined the invitation, saying I couldn't afford it and even if I could, I would much rather visit Stonehenge.

We sat around the kitchen table, sharing supernatural experiences, and I shared one I had years before that I believed played a part in my excommunication with the church: "I saw dark angels—or shadows, as I call them—provoking Pastor Jacob to frustration and then he kicked me out."

One of the women asked, "Why, after receiving the vision, did you continue to walk away from God?"

I attempted to explain what I was still trying to figure out myself. "I spoke with Pastor John about my visions, and he told me they weren't from God. He said, if anything, it was probably the enemy and I shouldn't entertain them."

Joan went on to explain how they had limited understanding of the spiritual realm back then but had learned a lot since. While I was glad for their spiritual growth, I couldn't help but be frustrated—mainly at myself, realizing the visions God showed me during my season of witchery had been written off as deception. My heart had told me I was receiving revelation from God, but my intellect had been influenced by my faith in church authority.

As I prepared to leave, Joan gave me a Mother's Day CD that included an Amy Grant song that reminded her of me. I put the CD in the stereo when I got home, and listened to the song, which made me realize I had missed out on an entire decade with them.

Large U-Haul trucks were parked in front of Pastor John and Joan's home when I pulled up the next day. This was it, moving day. Men carried pieces of furniture out of the house, which was already beginning to feel empty. I worked with a few women, rolling carpets and taking apart furniture. We removed curtains and packed any remaining items. I helped take apart a bed frame that would be sent over to the house where John and Joan would be staying for the next six months until they officially moved.

Joan came into the room where I was working, carrying a package that had just been delivered. She opened the wrapping and pulled out a tabret adorned with sparkling red, orange, and gold streamers. The center was of gold cloth with gold sequins forming a cross. Along each side of the cross there were flaming wings of fire. "This specific tabret was used in praise and worship and represented the Holy Spirit Fire," Joan explained. Then she handed it to me. "I hope to hear about you using this in worship."

Holding the beautiful tabret, I began reading the Scripture verses that came along with it pertaining to the Holy Spirit. I wasn't completely sure of God's purpose, but I knew His hand was at work even in the giving of this gift.

We went back to packing until the house was empty. The elders had been there much of the day helping load the trucks, and once it was done, they retreated to the basement for a brief meeting and time of prayer. I looked around the empty home that was so full of memories. I had met Michael there in the kitchen, and we had our first dinner together in that dining room. Many times I sat there in the family room looking through the bay window and listening to Joan play the piano.

I walked out on the deck, which had been built during the time I had been away. This was the first chance I had to see it. Looking over the field that led to a small lake, I remembered the time Michael and I had walked back there with John and Joan to talk and pray. I went back in through the kitchen, found my purse and new tabret, took one more look around the house, and then walked out on a piece of my history for the last time.

CHAPTER TWENTY-THREE

—ᗯᗯ—

A t church, I felt empty. It was a time of adjustment within the church, as well as in my personal life. Accepting the consequences for your actions is not an easy task.

When John and Joan returned for a short visit, they took me out for lunch. What a blessing to share this precious time with them. We talked about what God had done, but the focus didn't remain there. Pastor John talked to me about using the gifts God had given me for His purpose and kingdom. It was difficult to grasp that God could have a purpose in His kingdom for me, and I was a bit fearful at the thought.

Weeks later, I was caught off guard at what should have been a normal Sunday service. Pastor Jacob was sharing a message about God's calling for some to pick up and go. I sensed by the way the message was going that it was leading to a personal announcement, and I was right.

Pastor Jacob and Liz would be placing their home up for sale, as he had accepted an offer for another job out of state. As if it wasn't hard enough to deal with Pastor John's leaving, now I was losing the comfort of knowing that he and Liz were still there. They knew me, and knew about the circumstances concerning Michael. Their home had been a refuge where I could run when the unpleasantness of my home situation became overwhelming. The end of the service brought more tears as yet another goodbye was at hand.

So came more work days to help prepare their home for the market. I helped with painting the woodwork in the living room, where I had attended prayer meetings while contemplating why I had come. In the room sat the piano Pastor Jacob had often used to play the song that had always brought tears to my eyes, "Create in Me a Clean Heart," and at the table in the adjoining dining room, young mothers in the church had made the banner that still hung in the church. That was the first thing I'd seen on my first Sunday back in church.

Working together on that piece of cloth had not only created a banner but also a bond between those who created it. All the women had moved on except Liz, and now she was leaving as well. My children had played in the basement with theirs during many prayer meeting nights, and now my children were troubled teens not knowing what to believe in.

I was standing on a ladder, brushing fresh paint on the woodwork around the ceiling, when a secular rock song came on the radio. I stopped painting and listened, awaiting a dispute over the music but heard none.

Liz, who was painting across the room, looked over at me. "Is there something wrong?"

"Well, kind of," I said, "I thought rock music was evil."

She half smiled. "We listen to rock music."

"Well, how come I got the third degree when I went to a Fleetwood Mac concert way back when?" I asked.

"We're just careful who's around when we listen to it," she replied.

I smiled but thought it hypocritical as I remembered Pastor John's and Michael's madness to restrain me from a concert and Michael's refusal to allow me to listen to rock in my own home. For the first time, I began to see Pastor Jacob and Liz in a mortal way and realized we all had skeletons in our closet. In a strange way, our time working together on a common project brought some resolution in my Christian relationships.

When the work for the day was through, we sat out on the front porch and talked about their move and our seasons of change. It looked as if I would have no alternative but to rely less on man and more on God.

I had been so busy helping people move that I hadn't much time to keep in touch with the coven. That was, until Amber was able to reach me and informed me I was expected to be at the next Friday-night ritual since I'd missed quite a few.

I stopped at the store to pick up something for the feast, then called Bo en route to let him know I was going, already contemplating the argument I would receive. Deep down I believed his arguments to defend God were really his excuse to manipulate and control, but, fearing another rejection, I didn't want to confront him. I had no sooner said I was going to ritual when Bo went off.

"How can you treat Him this way?" he demanded. "We've done all we could to get you back into a right place with God, and you so easily turn your back on Him!"

"Why are you taking this so personally? This is between God and me. It would be far better if you'd stop trying to be Him and let God be God. He certainly knows how to handle me better than you ever could."

"He doesn't want you worshiping other gods."

"Then let Him deal with me on that."

"I bet you haven't told Pastor Lyndon where you're going tonight."

"I haven't had the chance."

"Well, he'll know about it, I can tell you that much."

"You're threatening to call him? Don't bother. I'll make the call for you!" I flipped the phone shut. I had planned on talking to Pastor Lyndon the next day but figured I'd best call him right away.

"While I certainly am not encouraging you to go, I know you hear God and would trust Him to speak to you in His timing," he said when I explained that I was on my way to a ritual. He went on to emphasize that he had never said I should turn my back on my friends but the day would come when I might want to share my God-encounter with them. Then he prayed with me. Surprisingly, there was no yelling or arguing. This "it's in God's hands" attitude was one I didn't quite know how to respond to, but I could see God working through it.

The shop door was locked, and I had to knock to be let in. When Amber opened the door, the room was already smoky from the incense and the altar had been set up and arranged.

"About time you showed up!" she said.

I hugged her. "It's been a while, I know."

"Are you okay?"

"There's a lot going on," I admitted, "but I'm okay."

"Goddess will take care of you. I need you here."

I smiled and put the covered dish I brought on the table as the rest of the coven filled the room. After being away, it was good to see everyone again. Amber called me outside to discuss our ritual with the high priest, then we returned and Amber announced it was time to robe.

The coven sat in a circle to ground as I retreated to another room with Amber and easily slipped back into my role as hand-maiden. She put her Goddess garment over her head and turned around for me to fasten it. "Can you grab the face paint in the bag over there?" She pointed to a large silver bag on the floor.

I fumbled through it until I found the paint and handed it to her. She took what she wanted and handed it back to me. We then painted our faces, sharing a few laughs in between sips of mead. Amber placed her circlet on her head and I tied it in place, then we took a few minutes to do our own grounding, making ourselves ready for entering sacred space.

I opened the door and walked out, lit the candles on the altar, and motioned the drummers to begin. A few seconds later, Amber walked in and the ritual began. Magic filled the air, and as we danced deosil, or clockwise around the circle, I could feel the energy rising.

Then a large, unimaginable tongue of fire swept down from heaven and consumed the sacred space. Its fiery glow terrified me as it lingered, continuing to burn in the center of our circle. My hands shook as I took a deep breath, trying to compose myself. When I looked at the other coveners, none gave any indication that they'd witnessed it.

I tried to process what I just experienced. Flaming tongues of fire are referenced in the Bible, but what would one be doing here? My focus was distracted by words that pierced my soul: "Where you are, there I am also."

I was paralyzed by the thought of God being in the circle. My mind raced so much that I couldn't refocus on the magic being worked. Time seemed to stand still until Amber told us to release the quarters. I can't remember the words I garbled and can only hope I didn't say something totally unintelligible.

Amber then closed the circle, and I attempted to brush off what had happened and join in the feasting. While I took only a small portion in an attempt to eat and run, one of the coven confronted me. Caught off guard, I wondered if she had seen my reaction to the tongue of fire.

"I want you to know you're a source of hope to me," she said. "You probably don't know this, but I was going through a difficult time and remember looking into your eyes to find strength and fire, wisdom and compassion."

In that instant, I recognized the eyes she described were not mine, but the eyes of Jesus! She had seen His eyes through mine at a time when I wasn't even walking with Him.

Trying to keep my composure, I embraced her and gently said, "Thank you. I'm always here for you."

With that, I threw my robe in my tote and hurried out the

door. I was driving home when Bo called my cell phone. I wouldn't have answered except I wanted to share the supernatural events that occurred. I began, "Before you go off, just listen to what I have to say."

Bo kept silent as I shared what had happened. When I was finished, he said, "Wow! You mean to say He was there, of all places? I know there's a part in the Bible that says, 'Where can I flee from your spirit? If I go to heaven or make my bed in hell, you are there.'"

I turned onto the road toward home. "I know, but reading it and seeing it are two different things! I'm going to hang up so I can digest this. Talk to you when I get home." I flipped my cell shut, tossed it on the passenger seat, and remorsefully prayed, "Okay, Lord. You've once again outdid yourself, and you truly are always with me, even in the most unexpected places."

—m—

The next time I went to a coven meeting, we shared a bitter-sweet time, as Orion had accepted a job offer out of state and would no longer be our high priest. I sat cross-legged among the others on the floor of the shop, listening to a few conveners questioning the uncertainty of the impending change, and seized the opportunity. "This is definitely a season of change," I said.

All eyes fixed on me, except for those of Amber, who entered notes in the coven Book of Shadows.

"In fact, it will never be the same again. Orion's departure will definitely be cause of an unbalanced polarity in our circle for a time, but he's not the only one leaving."

Amber looked up, her eyes focused on me.

"This will be the last time I'm here," I continued. "The only way I can explain it, is that I found a greater love that I simply cannot say no to."

"Ally, we'll talk about that later!" she cut me off before I could utter another word.

I don't know if they were in denial or if they understood who the source of this greater love was, but most of them looked totally bewildered. No one dared to question it, and I can't blame them. Amber had made it perfectly clear that this confession was not open for discussion.

A WITCH'S ENCOUNTER WITH GOD

CHAPTER TWENTY-FOUR

—⚭—

Worship was well under way as I hurried into church and stood in the back of the sanctuary, unable to find a seat. Looking out across the congregation, I saw the passion on people's faces as they lifted their hands in praise. I closed my eyes to reflect on God and saw a vision ...

Jesus in all His glory was riding upon a white horse. The white of His garments was brilliant in color and shone with such radiance that it was blinding. Then I saw thousands of angels with their gleaming wings reflecting His light, and thousands of people cloaked in white robes. Some were riding white horses, and some walked on foot. Amid a crowd of robes in many colors, I recognized the scepter of the Goddess being held in the air. These people rode gray horses, but some were walking. The two kingdoms were on opposing sides and their paths led to different destinations.

Feedback shrieked in the microphone, and I jerked and dropped my purse. The worship leader went on singing, but I couldn't, unable to get the vision out of my head. The revelation I received was that Wicca was not just another path; they were going in an entirely different direction. I had never perceived it this way before, thinking that all paths led to the same source. Now I realized there truly was a conflict between the two realms.

The song ended, closing worship, but it opened my mind to the possibility of the battle within.

—⚭—

A few weeks later, Pastor John returned to give a seminar on healing and deliverance. Rosa and Will came to attend, and it was a great opportunity to see them again. They stayed at the hotel where the seminar was being held, so we met for coffee before it began.

The morning consisted of an introduction, followed by the church's role in healing and deliverance. The first session concluded with the healing ministry of deliverance and the subject of whether a Christian could be oppressed by demons. On our break, we mingled with others from the seminar and overheard a conversation regarding the stereotypical Halloween horrors.

"We need to pray against cats being sacrificed and babies being snatched by witches and warlocks!" an ill-informed woman passionately pled.

Rosa cringed, and I bit my tongue for fear of saying the wrong thing.

As we headed back to the conference room, Will asked, "Ally, how are you dealing with what you just heard about Halloween?"

By now, I had regained my composure. "I'm more concerned with pagans that don't know Jesus after hearing her misguided comments!"

Rosa interjected, "This is where you need to be the one to extend God's grace to His people, because they really don't know."

The afternoon topics consisted of freedom from occult influences, which was a hot topic for us. They gave a laundry list of influences, ranging from the obvious such as divination and astrology to the humorous such as cartoons and Star Wars. At this point, I could check off almost the entire list!

The seminar then turned to the scriptural pattern for healing and deliverance, which consisted of identifying the strongman, discerning demonic influences, and casting them out. Overall, the seminar was a good experience, and Rosa used this opportunity to set up a time to return for deliverance prayer. That night, we went to a nice country restaurant for dinner.

That's when I got a call from Lynn. "Mom! Dad is going crazy!" she told me.

I could hear Michael shouting and things breaking. "What's going on?" I asked. My heart pounded at the violent rage in the background.

"He pushed me into the refrigerator!" she cried.

"Go to your room and lock the door. I'm on my way!" I hung up the phone.

By the time I arrived home, Michael was lying quietly on the couch. I found Lynn, who was physically unharmed, but the emotional damage was already done.

As time went on, I slipped into my own state of depression. The continuation of this living arrangement was taking its toll, as I struggled to find peace and happiness in a home with a manic-depressive who thrived on negativity. Pastor John and Joan had come for another visit, so I had the opportunity to speak with him after the service. Realizing the volatile state I was in, he called for Pastor Lyndon and arranged for me to meet with the women of the church on days there wasn't a prayer meeting so I could be out of the home and in fellowship.

Pastor Lyndon led the next Thursday-night prayer meeting since Pastor Timothy was out of town. Afterward, I sat at the kitchen table talking with him about my walk. We discussed my reluctance to go all out for God, and Lyndon asked if I feared retaliation from the coven, reassuring me of God's protection. I wasn't concerned with potential physical danger, since I knew my coven better than that. They might have thought I was totally crazy for returning to the ways of the Christian God, but the choice was mine to make.

I wasn't expecting anything like the horror stories I had heard about when others had attempted to leave. It wasn't like that at all, not with Wicca and certainly not with the group I was involved in. However, the spiritual plane was another story. The Goddess I had worshiped and vowed to serve had a dark side. Any fear I had concerned that realm.

Pastor Lyndon suggested a prayer for deliverance again, and at this point I accepted the fact that the day for that was fast approaching.

CbAPTER TWENTY-FIVE

—⚏—

At three a.m. the house was silent except for the normal creaking of an old house and the snoring of Cujo. I awoke to the radio, which for some odd reason had begun to play a song about an angel. Half asleep, I reached for the off button and realized the radio wasn't even on.

I sensed something strange in my surroundings, but I didn't quite know what, and I was too tired to figure it out. Then a simple thought came to me: pray for God to send His angels. So, I prayed, amazed at the words that came forth from my lips as I asked for God's fiery angels— warring angels to come. Not having any idea what a warring or fiery angel was or if there was such a thing, I continued to pray until I felt a complete peace and drifted back to sleep.

When the feast of Rhiannon approached, I came home from work to find Luna sitting in distress on the bottom of her cage. I picked her up and noticed her breathing was heavy, so I called the veterinarian and was told to bring her right in. The office was an hour away, and after finding an appropriate box, I carefully placed Luna in it before heading out to the car. Lynn came along with me to hold her while I drove.

We hadn't even reached the highway when the sound of fluttering wings drew our attention to the box. Luna was attempting to take flight in the small enclosed space. Suddenly her fluttering stopped as she lay over and took her last breath. Lynn sat silently with tears running down her face.

I turned the car around and headed for home, attempting to

hold back the tears of grief over the death of my fine feathered friend. She had been with me for nine years, joining me in circle and always nearby when I was working magic.

Her burial needed to be special, so I placed some bedding in a sturdy file box with gold suns and moons and found the spot that would be her grave. As the box was lowered and then covered with the dirt, I heard these words: "I am the maker of the birds. It is I who gives life and it is I who takes it away. Remember this."

"Rhiannon," I said softly. This was her day, and she was the goddess of the birds. Her message—her warning was clear to me that she who had given, in her dark aspect could also destroy. A flood of emotions raged through me. There was anger that my feathered friend was gone, for no other reason than to prove the sovereignty of the Goddess. Yet even in my anger, I somehow accepted it as a cost but asked what else would be taken away.

That prompted a call to Pastor Lyndon, who told me, "I know you don't like the term demonic, so let's just say there are 'other sources' that aren't exactly happy with your turning back to God. What you have to remember is that God is all powerful. Satan is on a leash and can only go as far as God allows him. God will protect you from anything the enemy can throw at you."

"You forget I'm one of *her* own."

"You are a child of God Almighty!" he countered. "You were a Christian long before any goddess was in the picture. Jesus bought you with His blood on the cross, and Scripture says nothing, not death nor hell nor demons, can separate you from the love of God."

After Pastor Lyndon prayed for me, he suggested I attend the intercessory prayer meeting that night. I had tried to stay away from intercessions, as they were a likely place for spiritual warfare, but I stopped over for fellowship at the home of a deaconess and mentioned the intercessory prayer meeting. She told me that if Pastor Lyndon had suggested it, there must be a reason for me to be there. She also told me that Pastor John and Joan were to be the focus of the prayer that evening, as they were transitioning into their new home.

That night, we walked into the church and found our seats near the front, not my usual choice of seating. I preferred sitting in the back and had just about decided to move when Joan came over. We spoke a bit before the meeting began, and then the pastors explained that Pastor John and Joan had moved into an area where they felt they were being oppressed by a heavy witchcraft influence.

I sunk in my chair, thinking this is not where I wanted to be. They called everyone to join hands in a circle to pray in unity, but I remained in my seat since I really didn't want to be a part of it. One of the men noticed me sitting on the sideline and called out for me to join them, making room for me in the circle. I reluctantly got up and joined hands as the voices of the saints turned from spiritual tongues to spiritual warfare.

Now I really wanted to leave, but once again Joan approached me. "Will you stand in the gap?" she asked. "With your having been caught up in witchcraft, will you stand in that place? God can really use you in this."

"Oh no. I'm sorry, Joan," I said. "I can't go there."

"What are you afraid of?" another voice asked.

"I'm not afraid."

"There's nothing to fear. God is with you."

"It's not that."

"What is it then?" Joan asked.

"We need to pray against this fear," someone declared.

Before I knew it, those around me were laying hands on me and praying.

As the praying grew louder, I realized the entire focus of the prayer was directed toward me, not Pastor John. I looked up to see that I was overtaken by a flash mob of prayer warriors. I panicked and felt trapped like a caged animal. Pastor Lyndon and Pastor John were nowhere to be found. I kept hoping for them to come save me, as I felt like steam in a boiling kettle with no way out. A woman's voice kept crying out, praying over and over, "For the love of Jesus, for the love of Jesus!"

I felt as though I would explode and began pushing back the crowd. "Where are they?" I cried.

Then I heard a familiar voice coming from alongside of me with a prayer that was soft and comforting. I recognized it as Pastor Lyndon's, and then I heard Pastor John on the other side. Then I felt something break, and there was some kind of release. Here I had been searching for these two men to come to my rescue, not knowing they were right at my side and were in fact part of those praying warriors. Pastor John told people to back off and give me space.

The prayer meeting ended, though we never did get to pray for Pastor John and Joan. It seemed God had another plan for that night. I felt like I had been picked up in a spiritual tornado, spun around, and then placed on totally different ground. Something had most definitely changed.

I spoke with Pastor Lyndon about it the next day.

"Are you all right with the prayer last night?" he asked. "I have to tell you I didn't plan that."

"I know it wasn't planned. I kept looking around for you and Pastor John to come rescue me, but I couldn't find you."

"I was praying across the room when someone interrupted me, saying I should know they started praying for you. I thought they just meant you were getting prayer, so I went into the office and was fumbling through some music. When I came over to pray for you, I was behind everyone."

"I didn't know you were there until I heard your voice and realized you and Pastor John were both right there with me." I looked him in the eye. "Something happened though. It was like something broke. There was something with you two both being there. I don't understand it."

"I was standing in the back because I couldn't reach you with everyone around," he explained. "Someone approached me with a vision they had of me standing next to you. I called for John, and we made our way through to stand alongside of you."

"I don't remember half of what happened. It's like my mind is blank. I remember the beginning when they started praying, someone praying for the love of Jesus, and then your voice and finally John's. Why don't I remember any of it?"

"I wouldn't worry about that. God's ways are not our ways, and He had your deliverance planned for last night," he concluded.

The days following brought no new revelation of what happened that night. I gathered bits and pieces from those that were there. People told me I was trying to push away from Pastors Lyndon and John, which seemed unlike me since I respected both men and had looked for them to rescue me. And why had I felt like I needed rescuing? Unsettling as it was, I knew what had happened was from God and I was at peace with it.

A WITCH'S ENCOUNTER WITH GOD

CHAPTER TWENTY-SIX

—⁓—

Each year, New Zion held a woman's conference—a weekend event of teaching, prayer, and fellowship. The time for the conference had come, and I was apprehensive about going, considering the instability at home. I never knew what behavior to expect from Michael, but after assurance from the elders to put my trust in God, I joined the other women.

After the evening session was over, the guest pastor remained up front for those who came forward. Joan walked me to the front area, which was now filled with women waiting to receive prayer. A sense of fear overcame me, though I didn't know what I was afraid of. Around me, women were being slain in the Spirit, or so overcome by the presence of God that they fell to the ground. I was glad Joan stood beside me with her arm wrapped around my shoulder. Over the praying voices, I heard what sounded like a woman groaning in labor. Even though I had seen things in the Spirit, this was all new to me.

As the pastor approached me, that familiar lump in my throat indicated my panic. He took my hands and held them in his, and immediately I felt peace flow through me. His eyes were compassionate, and his gentle soft-spoken words soothed my weary soul. I don't remember all he said, but I do remember him speaking about my hurt being so deep that not even tears could come from my eyes. His eyes then filled with tears as he began to pray for me. I didn't understand what he meant by my not being able to cry, thinking perhaps I had cried all my tears out over the past few months.

Even so, I left the seminar with a song on my lips and joy in my heart.

—⟋⟍—

When I returned home, the household appeared intact, but something had changed with my children. It was as though they had withdrawn and the closeness wasn't there. My being away had caused them to seek refuge away from their father. Lynn had left the tension of home for her friend's house where she was spending more time. She had also been stretching her curfew, and pushed me away as I bore the brunt of her understandable anger. Likewise, Aaron was practically living next door with his friend, wrapped up in computer games and fantasy, and Missy escaped to a neighboring community called The Orchards with her network of high school friends.

Our family had become a replica of Michael's. I had hoped my children would grow up in a loving home environment like I had, but instead we lived under the influence of a dysfunctional union of manipulation. Over the years, I had become somewhat numb to Michael's rejection and ridicule, even learning to ignore the sound of his roar as he made his annoyance known. My children, though, had suffered greatly from both his roar and his bite. Seeing how Michael's condition had turned everyone against each other broke my heart.

—⟋⟍—

One night as I sat up waiting for Lynn, I realized the year before it had been her sitting up waiting for me to come home. While I was off trying to escape our unhealthy home life in magical space or the refuge of Bo's arms, my children were at home waiting. Why hadn't I removed them from this environment long ago?

Now I watched as they clung to whatever escape rope they could find. As I prayed for my children, I kept hearing, "Love them unconditionally." God impressed on my heart not to use discipline but continuous love. I knew the effects His unconditional love had on me, so I trusted that love was indeed the answer. Long ago, Pastor John had said he had heard a similar thing when praying about me; God told him to simply love me. The testimony of God's unconditional love was evident in my life, so I trusted it would be in my children's as well.

Exhausted from another sleepless night, I made my way out back with Cujo at my side. I collapsed in the tree hammock and cried out to my heavenly Father, asking forgiveness for all the times I had left my children in the anxiety of the home for my own selfish desires. Cujo nudged my hand and put his head in my lap as I grieved for all I had done.

I called Pastor Lyndon, who reminded me that while it was good for me to recognize the error of my ways, I also needed to realize that Michael had a part to play in all of this. He had disregarded his God-appointed position as head of the family, leaving me to attempt to fill a role that was designed to be his. There was a large void in my children's life that was not my doing, since their father had just as much responsibility for their present mind-set as I did. Though they were responsible for the choices they were making, their father's lack of fathering and the constant instability of our household had severely impacted them.

One Saturday afternoon, after a particularly long night, I became so overwhelmed by the spiritual, physical, and emotional turmoil, that I called Pastor Timothy. After I told him what I was going through, he made what I thought to be a strange suggestion: "I think one of the things you need to do is get rid of those things you're still holding onto regarding Wicca."

"You mean the books, tools, and stuff?" I asked.

"I know it will be hard for you, but you need to let go of these things once and for all. You're being pulled because you're still holding onto your past."

"What does any of that have to do with my children and my home situation?"

"It has to do with your making a choice to go God's way," he patiently explained. "By putting your past behind you, I believe it will free you from feeling torn between Wicca and Christianity. Things in your family life will start to fall into place once you get your life in godly order."

"Lyndon mentioned that before," I confirmed.

"I believe you will see things turn around once you put yourself in a place of blessing," Pastor Timothy reassured me before ending the conversation with a word of prayer.

The next day, I opened the trunk and placed the linen-wrapped pentacle inside. Then after slamming the door shut, I headed for the church. Pastor Lyndon stood near the door, greeting people as they entered. I handed back his keys, and he smiled as I walked into the sanctuary.

I don't know what he did with it, and I never asked.

—m—

Late one afternoon, I pulled into my driveway. Opening the gate to the backyard, I met my laundry, which was hanging out to dry. "Whoa, those are dark!" I stopped, not believing what I'd just said.

As I looked at my ritual robes, I noticed a darkness I had never seen before. The robes were black, but color was not the darkness I was sensing. Amazing that such a thought would come to mind! I quickly pulled them off the line and carried them inside.

The time had come for me to take the next step. After finding an empty box, I filled it with books, clothing, and other magical paraphernalia. The handmade tools were the hardest to place in the box, as a lot of my own energy had gone into their making.

On Sunday, I told Pastor Lyndon about the box that I had brought to turn over to him.

"Hallelujah," he said and handed me the keys to his car once again. Before I walked away, he asked, "Is that everything?"

I was tempted to say yes, but I had to be honest. "There are three things I feel I can keep," I told him. "A drum that I never used for ritual, the staff I was working on that isn't completed, and my Book of Shadows, which is a mirror of my past."

Pastor Lyndon considered that, then concluded, "Pray about those things and see if God would really have you hold on to them."

I hated it when he calmly told me to go pray about something. He was leaving me to wrestle with God over it, yet at the same time I knew leaving God to deal with me was simply the best way to handle it. I tried to convince myself that I had good reasons for holding onto these things, but when I stood before God, my actions no longer seemed justifiable.

Soon I was driving up Pastor Lyndon's driveway with another box in my car.

He came out to meet me, then led me around to an iron fire pit in the backyard. "Are you sure you want to do this?"

I nodded and handed over the box.

After placing it in the area meant for firewood, he set it on fire.

I stood watching the flames consume things that I considered a part of my life, yet I viewed the fire's dance as sacred.

When the fire died down, he looked at the book I held in my hands. "Do you want to do that one too?"

"My Book of Shadows," I said as I clasped it tighter. "Well, maybe I should keep it so I can use it for my testimony." I searched his face for approval, but he just stood there waiting. After a few moments, I knew I had to complete the task I had set out to do. Taking a deep breath, I handed it over. "Yes, I can do this."

He nodded. "I think you should."

I stepped closer to the flames and tossed in my Book of Shadows, which quickly caught fire. All my magical workings, spells, rituals, poetry, and writings went up in smoke. The staff was the last to be consumed by the fire, and I prayed that my life would now move into some semblance of order.

CHAPTER TWENTY-SEVEN

—⁂—

I walked into a small waiting room in a rather large apartment complex. After checking in with the receptionist, I sat on the couch and took cover behind a *Good Housekeeping* magazine. A Christian song playing on the radio, and I lifted my eyes from the page I wasn't reading and glanced over at a bookshelf full of books on assorted topics.

Within a few moments, a tall, dark-haired man walked in the room. "Hello," he said as he extended his hand. "I'm Phil, the counselor you spoke with over the phone. Come on back this way." He led me to an office tucked in a corner at the end of the hallway. "Take a seat wherever you'd like."

One wall of the room was covered with mirrors that made me a bit self-conscious, but there was also a comfortable-looking couch. Next to a row of windows sat a bookshelf, a desk, and a chair. I chose the chair by the door across from the desk. Though the couch may have been more comfortable, it reminded me of the whole shrink thing.

"Let's start with some basic information about you, and then I'll explain the practice here," Phil began.

We went through the formalities of my personal information, and he explained the financial guidelines. I applied for charity assistance since I was unable to afford counseling, and he told me that process could take several months. With that finished, he addressed my reason for coming. I briefly explained the spiritual, physical, and emotional dilemmas that had led to my being depressed. He asked more questions, then suggested I go to my physician to be sure there wasn't an underlying physical reason for my mental state and to see if medication might go along with his therapy.

The hour and a half was over quickly, and to my surprise he scheduled my next session right away even though the charity assistance hadn't yet been approved.

—◊◊◊—

Though I was taking steps to deal with my own depression, the nightmare at home continued to make me feel like I was carrying the weight of my entire household. My days at work were filled with anxiety as I wondered how things were at home.

One day, my boss came to my desk and told me there was a call on line two for me. My heart raced, anticipating something was wrong. Lynn's friend who lived a few doors down blurted out, "Lynn asked me to call you because she's afraid of her dad and he cut the phone wires!"

Everything went blank and then I thought the worst. Swallowing the lump in my throat, I said, "I'll be right there!" and told my boss I had an emergency at home.

I ran down the stairs to my car. It seemed I caught every red light as I raced home. As I pulled up, Michael was hurrying to the car as he held Missy by the arm.

I got out and heard Lynn's screaming from her bedroom window. "Where are you going?" I demanded of Michael.

Missy stood next to him, teary-eyed, as she bit her lip.

"We're getting out of here," Michael said before mumbling something about Lynn being just like me.

I took Missy's other arm and pulled her toward me. "You can go, but Missy is staying here with me."

Michael attempted a tug of war over our daughter, but I wasn't backing down. "Get in my car," he said to Missy.

"No!" I insisted.

"Mom, I don't know what to do," Missy whimpered.

"Missy, listen to me." I locked eyes with her. "Come behind me, sweetheart. We're going inside." I stepped between the two of them and shouted, "Michael, let go of her! You can come back later once you've calmed down."

He released her, and I hurried Missy inside. After latching the door, I turned to find Aaron pacing the living room. "Take Missy up to your room!" I instructed and then hurried upstairs to Lynn.

She was hysterical but physically unharmed. "Missy and I were arguing," she explained. "I don't remember why, but dad rushed in and grabbed me by the neck. I pulled away and went for my cell to call you, but he took my phone and started downstairs. I went for the house phone, but before I could dial your number, the phone went dead. I heard him coming back upstairs and looked out the window. I saw Carly and called for help."

—⁂—

Nights brought a level of anxiety that kept me awake and driving aimlessly for hours, unable to sit or keep my mind from constant worry.

The day of my doctor's appointment for my physical finally arrived, and once the test results came back, I was put on thyroid medication and the antidepressant Zoloft. I continued my counseling sessions with Philip as well as spiritual counseling with Pastor Lyndon.

One day, I returned home from shopping to find the pastors of New Zion at my house. They had come to speak with Michael about our home situation, and Pastor John asked me to step outside so we could discuss what Michael had shared. "Ally, Michael said you've been spending all his money on phone calls to your boyfriend and the phone is being disconnected," he said.

I was shocked.

"He said no matter what you tell us, you've never stopped contact with Bo or tried to give your marriage another chance."

I didn't know if Michael had fabricated a story or if he was delusional and believed what he said. I responded, "The only phone I use is the cell that Bo gave me, and he pays the bill. Michael doesn't pay a dime. I was out of contact with Bo a year or so ago for the three months I promised you I would be, and Michael showed no signs of interest."

"Michael said he had no desire to work things out," he said.

The pastors told Michael it was time for him to make a decision about our marriage and that Pastor Lyndon would visit him in a week for his final answer.

After they left, my depressed state of mind dropped even lower. The torment of Michael's isolated world was infringing on mine. I just wanted out of this living hell that a piece of paper kept me bound to and finances kept me from undoing. The temptation for a money spell was intense, but I couldn't go there, not if I were to do this in a godly way.

When Pastor Lyndon knocked on our door a week later, Michael simply disappeared, refusing to give his final decision. In doing so, he made his decision more than obvious to all of us. Soon after, Pastor Lyndon met me at the lawyer's office, where we discussed the situation at home and what was needed to proceed with a divorce. Even though the lawyer had significantly lowered his fees, divorce still wasn't financially feasible. One thing that I did get from our meeting was yet another person telling me it was detrimental to my and my children's well-being to remain in our home environment. The years had taken more of a toll on me than I fully understood. I had become numb to how bad things really were, but now I sensed an urgency to act.

We left the lawyer's office and I returned home, where I suggested that Michael move out on his own. His stubborn refusal made me more determined than ever that divorce was not only desirable but crucial.

—∞—

After a few months on my medication, my situation began to look brighter even though things were still very much unsettled. I no longer experienced severe anxiety, I slept better, and there were even days when I was happy. I was also encouraged by the emotional and spiritual healing taking place in my daughters' lives.

One night, I drove up to the apartment complex where Lynn was waiting on the porch steps. She hopped in the passenger seat, clearly in a serious mood. As I pulled away, she began talking. "Mom, I'm sorry for staying out late and making you upset, but I can't help it when I'm so angry about things at home."

I listened as she opened up for the first time in a long time.

"I don't understand why dad is so mad at me all the time."

I sighed and tried to explain. "It's me he's angry with, and I'm sorry he takes it out on you kids."

Lynn fumbled with the CDs in the glove box. "I blame you, Mom."

For a second I was taken back. How was I to blame for Michael's behavior?

"Dad got worse when you started talking with Bo," she went on. "He showed me one of your emails. You can't blame him for being mad. I don't understand why you stayed, Mom. Why didn't you take us away from this?"

How could I explain my reasons for remaining in a dysfunctional household? "I understand you're hurt, and I would have done anything to keep you from this. It's not easy financially to just pick up and move, but I'm so sorry, Lynn." We pulled up to the front of the house, and Lynn got out and went inside while I went to park the car.

Our open, honest conversation meant more to me than words could ever say. From then on, things started getting better between us.

Then Missy came home and told me, "I just joined a Bible club at school. We meet Wednesdays after school for an hour, and I need you to sign this so I can go." She handed me a permission form, which I happily signed. "Oh yeah, and can I go on the youth retreat that Megan's youth group is having in the mountains?"

I smiled. "Sure you can, but I need details about the trip."

God was definitely answering my prayers for my children. At last I experienced some semblance of peace.

—⁂—

October brought the colors of fall and the smell of autumn leaves. Samhain was fast approaching, but though I received an invitation, I declined attending the ball. When I had stayed home from rituals in the past, every essence of my being longed to be there and I always felt like I was missing out on something. This time, the night of the ball came and went without any regrets as did the actual day of Samhain. In fact, I reveled in the release I experienced. The connected thread in the web had been broken, and I was free at last. Or so I thought.

The Christmas season brought the decorations and lights that always seemed to warm the cold nights of winter. I anticipated this year being a joyful occasion of celebrating the birth of Jesus within the fellowship of believers.

On the Sunday before Christmas, I walked in to church to find it transformed into a scene of old Jerusalem. Everyone was busy with the final touches of the Christmas musical, and I sat alone as the children came out for their performance. Following the grand finale of a host of angels singing, and watched as people cheerfully exchanged hugs, Christmas cards, and gifts, I got up and walked through the noisy crowd and out the door without anyone taking notice.

A few days later came Yule. This was the first time in years that I wasn't celebrating with the coven. Amber always decorated elaborately for the holidays, and I could almost smell the pine needles from the Yule tree decorated with suns, moons, and stars. Instead of my black velvet dress, I was wearing jeans and a sweatshirt. By now, we would have lit the Yule log and exchanged our gifts. But I sat solemnly on my couch and watched the twinkle of my own Christmas tree. I missed conversing with the coven and the way we sat around the fire laughing and making merry. I felt like one falling snowflake disappearing unto the winter landscape.

I realized this lack of fellowship could be detrimental to my walk. God had made me the type of person who did best with close friendships, something that had not happened at New Zion. I called Pastor John to tell him I was considering checking out other churches where I might fit in. He listened to my reasoning and said it wasn't a bad idea, but he cautioned that I should be sure to attend the midweek meetings and let Pastor Lyndon know what I was doing. Then he told me he felt it was important that I use the gifts God had given me no matter what church I might be in. He believed I would not be satisfied until I did, and mentioned a few spiritual gifts he felt I should be utilizing. After we had hung up, I realized that a move was what I needed, but not necessarily a physical move to another church. What I really needed was to move in the Spirit.

A WITCH'S ENCOUNTER WITH GOD

CHAPTER TWENTY-EIGHT

—⁂—

When I called home to check in with my parents, Mom answered. We had just started talking about the kids when my dad interrupted, "Did you tell her about my weird dream?"

"Not yet. You tell her," Mom responded.

My dad took the phone. "I had a dream that I died and kept trying to get back but couldn't," he said. "It felt like someone or something was holding me back and then I woke up."

I got an uneasy feeling in my gut.

"I guess I didn't make it back," he went on. "What do you think it means?"

I switched the phone to my other hand so I could shake off my clammy skin, and tried my best to be comforting. "I'm sure it was just a dream, Dad, and besides, as long as you're right with God, what's the worry?" But I silently asked its meaning myself. Was it a prophetic dream from God or from another source—and better yet, should I be attempting to interpret it?

Dad finished, "Well, like I've always said, when it's your time to go, there's no stopping it." With that he handed the phone back to my mom.

Not even a week later, he went to the hospital for chest pain. After running several tests, they sent him home, noting that all appeared fine. Being it was Saturday, I debated if I should go down to see him or wait a day until our usual Sunday gathering. I called to see how he was.

Mom told me he was having breakfast and said to him, "Your

daughter wants to know how you're feeling."

"Much better," I heard him reply.

"He slept well," she added.

Figuring all was fine, I hung up after saying I'd see them tomorrow.

Only a few hours later, my sister called to tell me the ambulance was rushing Dad to the hospital. She met me at my house, and we began the hour-long drive to the hospital. Oddly, I felt no urgency despite the 911 emergency.

We walked into the emergency room and told the receptionist whom we were there to see. A few seconds later, a nurse escorted us through the double doors, but instead of taking us to his bedside, she softly said, "Your mom will be in shortly," as she led us into a private room.

Something was wrong, though I wasn't prepared to hear exactly what. Mom came in a few minutes later and told us Dad had passed away. From being sent home healthy the day before and feeling fine this morning, to being gone in such a short time seemed surreal. We hugged as she tearfully shared, "The ambulance crew had said all his vitals were fine, but I insisted they bring him here. During the fifteen-minute ambulance ride, he passed."

The days that followed were hard on all of us. It forced me to confront the afterlife before I had time to fully tackle conversion. I returned home from our planning session at the funeral parlor and took a break on the couch. I still couldn't make sense of Dad being sent home from the hospital with a good bill of health only to die the very next day.

The voice inside my head was as clear as can be: "You can talk with your dad and find out exactly what happened." I almost agreed, but then it dawned on me that communication with the dead was not God's way. I resisted the thought, but it returned with a vengeance. I was wounded, and this battle in my mind warranted no sympathy.

The tears burst like an overrun dam, and my sobs came between my gasps of breath. Then I got angry. How dare deception rob me of my grief? I felt forced into exploring what life after death really meant, even though I hurt too much to care. The struggle continued between the rest of Summerland before reincarnation and the peace of heaven with no more tears or pain.

And then there was Dad's dream. Was it prophetic revelation or occult foreknowledge? What spirit worked within me? I sat confused, upset and trying to make sense of it all.

A few days later, I spoke with Pastor Lyndon. The first thing he said to me was, "Ally, don't give in to any temptation to contact your dad, because it would only be a demon pretending to be him."

How did he know? I could've used that confirmation a few days earlier, but Lyndon said he was unable to reach me.

The day of the funeral came, and I felt as though I hadn't yet mourned due to everything I was still trying to put in perspective. Several people from church were there, including Pastor Lyndon. Michael never came, claiming he was sick. I lost all respect for him, as I thought he should have at least been there for the children and for everything my dad had done for him. The funeral was held in the Episcopal church where I had grown up and where my parents still attended. In some strange way, I still felt my father was with me, which confused me even more because I knew the Bible said his soul was long gone. What then was this presence I felt?

I began seeking solitude at the cemetery, not to visit my dad as I knew his spirit had gone on, but rather to find refuge from the pain and confusion raging within. I had fond memories of the family graveside from when I was a little girl and my dad would take us to our grandparent's graves. We would run up and down the steps to the stone monument—the same monument that I now sat on as I wrote, prayed, and sobbed over the ongoing spiritual battle that continued in my life.

At times, I sunk into such despair that I longed for eternal peace and began entertaining the thought of being with my dad. Then my cell phone would ring and snap me back to reality. Lynn would be on the phone, calling for food or a ride home, and I'd quickly be on my way.

One afternoon, I was walking among the headstones as I silently sung the words of a song from church, "Breathe," that were so relevant of my life. I was desperately lost without God. As I headed back to my car, I heard that still small voice within saying, "Why do you search for the living among the dead?"

The story of the resurrection came to mind, and I thought of how the angel had told Mary that Jesus had risen from the dead. It was time for me to do the same. It really was all about Him, and as hard as it seemed, I had hope for new life. It would get better in time.

I left that day, leaving my hopelessness behind.

—⟋⟍—

Five months later, I came home to find Michael's station wagon filled to the brim. I cupped my hands on the glass and looked through it, curious about what he had inside. A large tarp covered the entire cargo area.

Disappointed to find his contraband camouflaged, I went into the house to investigate. A barking Cujo and a hissing Chloe greeted me, both confidently standing their ground. I led Cujo to the yard as Lynn came downstairs to collect Chloe.

"Hi, Mom. Is Dad taking stuff to the flea market?" she asked.

"Not that I'm aware of. Why?"

"I woke up the other night and glanced out the window and saw Dad holding a flashlight, putting a tarp inside his car packed with stuff."

Knowing Michael's secretive history, I called Missy down to see if she had any insight into his covert operation.

"I thought you already knew," she said, then went on to tell me that he had found an apartment and planned on moving within the week.

While it was something I believed was best for all of us, I couldn't understand the way he was going about doing it. When did he plan on telling me? Would he just silently go away without so much as saying a word? Since he wasn't offering information, I asked him directly if he was moving out. He said he had found a place and had been moving what he wanted from the house to his new apartment.

I found myself filled with a sorrow I couldn't understand. Alone and scared, I wondered how I would support my family since I had just lost my job. Scripture then came to mind: "He knows your every need and will provide for you much greater than the sparrows in the field."

Pastor Lyndon was trying to get me to accept financial help so I could go back to counseling when Phil called to say the financial assistance I had requested had come through. God has perfect timing, providing exactly what I needed. I told Phil I would like nothing more than to find a remote cabin in the middle of the woods and spend the rest of my life there alone with God. Phil explained that God designed us to be a part of a body and, no matter how much I wanted to, I could not do it all on my own.

Wasn't this what I had been hoping for all along? Yet now I wasn't looking for fellowship, but seclusion.

A WITCH'S ENCOUNTER WITH GOD

CHAPTER TWENTY-NINE

—⚬⚬—

We barely had enough time to recover from the oppression that was over the household with Michael when I received a call from Children's Services. One of Missy's friends, Cyndi, had been removed from her home and needed a place to stay. I didn't think twice before accepting her in. Cyndi was sixteen, a year younger than Missy. She had short auburn hair, freckles, and a Goth-style edge.

It was past midnight by the time Children Services left, and Cyndi was wide awake and eager to talk. "My mom abandoned me when I was five, and my dad, who was a lot older, raised us. After my dad died, I was sent to live with my brother and his wife, and my sister went to live with Dee, a friend of our family." Cyndi twisted her hair with her fingers. "I can't believe my brother accused me of killing my dad and their dog."

With Cyndi being such a sweet, innocent young girl, these horrible accusations seemed unwarranted. "Cyndi, didn't your father die of a heart attack?" I asked.

She looked up and nodded.

"It's not your fault." My heart went out to her, knowing all that she'd been through.

Then she dropped a bombshell: "My brother abused me and forced me to watch dirty movies. I'm so glad you're letting me stay."

She quickly settled in as part of the family and started calling me Mom. The following Sunday, we had dinner and cake at my mom's to celebrate Missy's seventeenth birthday. Cyndi had missed her birthday on the day of her move, so we celebrated them both together. Missy was delighted with the new cell phone I got her and a set of keys to use our old car.

"Do I have a cell phone too?" Cyndi asked.

"All my kids receive a cell on the seventeenth birthday, so you'll have to wait until next year, but I do have a present for you," I explained and handed her a gift.

I could tell no gift would live up to her expectations as she quickly unwrapped it. She scrunched her nose without a word, not impressed with the Mudd jeans and tops. I thought she'd be happy to have something to wear since it would be a while before she would be able to get her own from her brothers' house. My entire family treated her as one of our own.

We then sat around the dining room table and talked. One thing that disturbed me was Cyndi's lack of emotion over the recent loss of her father. The only emotion she did show was hurt and anger toward her runaway mother.

Soon the oppressive heaviness that had lifted when Michael left, returned to our home. I asked God if He had placed her in my home or if it had been the enemy acting as an angel of light. I prayed about it but didn't get an answer.

Cyndi came running down the stairs holding her journal. "Mom, I thought I'd share a poem I wrote because I know how much you like to write."

I set down the towel I was folding and gave her my attention. "Sure, Cyndi. I'd love to read it. Let's go into the living room so I can put on my glasses." She followed me, and I took a seat next to the table lamp as I put my glasses on.

I read of a broken heart and an obsession with death. I became concerned, but that wasn't the worst of it. Soon I was reading about a knife being plunged into somebody's chest and the graphic description of the blood gushing forth. Refraining from alarm, I looked up from the journal to see Cyndi standing there wearing her dark makeup, black choker, bondage pants, and a smile. She eagerly awaited my opinion as though her writing portrayed a normal everyday event.

"Your poem is very creative and imaginative," I said, handing back her journal. "It's a bit dark though, don't you think? Why the bloodshed?"

As Cyndi closed the journal, the cover revealed a dark fairy. "It's what I like to write about. It's fiction," she said. "Thanks for reading it, Mom." Then she disappeared up the stairs.

It took months before Cyndi could get all her belongings, which included furniture, clothes, and teenage paraphernalia. Lynn agreed to switch rooms and give the larger room to Missy and her new foster sister. When I went upstairs to check on their progress, I noticed a book in a box of Cyndi's belongings—a book on magic and spells.

I almost opened it, but instead held it tightly as I contemplated what to do. Then I heard God's still small voice: "What will you do with this?" I had but a few seconds to decide, so with the book in hand, I turned to Cyndi. "Why do you have this book?"

"It's not mine," she quickly said. "My friend left it at my house a long time ago, and I don't even know what it's about."

"Really?" I asked. "You're telling me you don't know this is a book of spells and witchcraft?"

"No. I never read any of it."

"Well, then call your friend and we'll drive it over and return it to her." Even as I challenged her, I could see the truth written all over her face.

"I don't know her address, and I lost her phone number."

"Cyndi," I said firmly, "I cannot have books on witchcraft, magic, or spells in my home." I couldn't believe the words that had just come out of my mouth—the same words I'd heard from my husband and pastor years before. I felt like a complete hypocrite but said it anyway. "I'm going to take this book and get rid of it. Any time you would like to talk about your friend's involvement in witchcraft, I'll be glad to listen."

I took the book and headed downstairs. It was crucial that this book get out of my house and fast. The temptation was not only Cyndi's, but also my own.

—m—

The girls were ready to leave for school, and Missy, who was driving our old Corsica, lagged behind while Cyndi went outside to wait. Missy pulled me aside and told me that Cyndi had a history of cutting herself and had several daggers hidden in their room.

While the girls were at school, I went upstairs to take a look. I immediately found her stash beneath her bed, but a further search revealed over twenty of them hidden throughout the room. This was of double concern as it was not just a safety issue; these daggers had goddess handles and other magical implications. I gathered them all and put them in a box in the basement for the time being.

I struggled with the proper way to approach this, remembering all too well the day Michael met me at the back door with my notes on crystals. I really resented him going through my stuff, but that was exactly what I'd just done with Cyndi. *Still, this was different,* I tried to convince myself. After all, a parent has a responsibility to watch out for a child's well-being.

Hours later, I heard footsteps on the front porch and the screen door close. Missy and Cyndi both smiled and said, "Hi Mom," then Missy asked, "What's up?"

"Hi, girls." I then looked at Cyndi. "We need to talk."

Missy read my expression, said, "Okay, I'm outta here!" and ran upstairs.

"Cyndi, I went in your room today," I began. "I found your

daggers and want to know why you have them."

She stared at her feet. "They're for decoration, Mom."

"Decoration? Why would you decorate underneath your bed?"

"I just like the way they look." She continued to avoid eye contact.

"Are you cutting yourself?" I asked. "Let me see your arms and legs."

Cyndi showed me her arms, which only had faded scars, but when she reluctantly lifted her skirt, fresh cuts crossed her thighs.

"I'm going to call your social worker and see about getting you into some counseling. I want to help you stop this," I said. With the physical aspect out of the way, I confronted the spiritual. "Are you using any of these daggers in ritual?"

"No. I just think they're pretty."

"Okay, then you won't mind that I took them all away."

"Mom!" Cyndi protested.

"Cyndi, I'm giving you the benefit of the doubt because you don't know all the house rules, but now you do. Daggers aren't permitted in the house."

I wasn't convinced of her willingness to comply, but let it slide. The tables had turned, and it didn't seem that long ago that I was the one denying my involvement with witchcraft.

On a Saturday afternoon, Aaron picked Cyndi up at a nearby park where she had been visiting with the kids she used to babysit for.

"It was so nice seeing them again," she told me when she got home. "I was the only one Crystal would talk to when I was a camp counselor." She went on to explain that their mom had then asked her to babysit. "You have to meet Celeste, Mom. You're a lot alike."

Interested, I asked, "In what ways are we alike?"

"Well, you're both into celestial and supernatural things, and I think you would really like her."

Before I could reply, the phone rang, and it was Cyndi's boyfriend so she took the call.

I soon learned my intuition wasn't always right. At the grocery store, I ran into Dee, a longtime friend of Cyndi's family and the woman who was caring for Cyndi's sister. We started talking, and she confided that she had empathy for me since I was caring for Cyndi.

She described Cyndi as a heartless child without a conscience from an early age, then she told me the mysterious story about Cyndi's brother's dog: "Cyndi got the leash, put it on the little white dog's collar, and said she was taking him for a walk. Some time went by before she arrived back home, expressionless and dragging the lifeless dog behind her. Her explanation was, 'On the way home from Celeste's house, the dog just fell over and died.' Her brother and his wife were devastated since the dog hadn't been sick, and they didn't believe Cyndi's fictitious story. They had an autopsy done, and it showed that the dog was strangled and its feet were bloodied in its attempt to fight for its life."

I couldn't shake off the image of a defenseless animal, or the fact that the hands that ended its life belonged to a child who was living in my home. I tried to second-guess her reasoning and wondered if it was Cyndi's revenge for the horrible way they had treated her.

Knowing I had to take some positive action, I insisted on taking her to youth group and was pleased to learn that she enjoyed it. She started going to church with me regularly, and I noticed she smiled more as she began to read her Bible. Missy joined her whenever she had off from work.

Despite the godly influence, however, her rebellion continued. She wanted to make her own rules to abide by and ignored any others. When I went up to the girls' room to get the dirty laundry, I found another dagger. This one was one of a series of knives with dark fairies on the handles. A search produced fifteen more knives, as well as crystals and other occult paraphernalia. I pulled a box from under the bed and found a charm bag with a stone and herbs intact, spellwork that Cyndi had previously denied she knew anything about.

I emailed Pastor John explaining the critical situation. He quickly replied that I should give Cyndi every opportunity to turn around, but that if she didn't, she should be removed from our home. I was faced with implementing Matthew 18 in my own household.

How could I consider kicking her out of my home, knowing what that had done to me? Would God use this situation to show me what it was like for my own spiritual father?

—⟋⟍—

During my prayer time, I read a verse that gave me direction on what to do: "They overcame him by the blood of the Lamb and by the word of their testimony" (Revelation 12:11 NKJV). It spoke to me in a powerful way and gave me insight into overcoming the temptation that still plagued me at times.

I was certainly covered with the blood of Jesus, but the one thing I hadn't done was share my testimony. I wanted to shout it from the rooftops, yet when I felt prompted to give my testimony at a prayer meeting, I couldn't even get the words out of my mouth. I shared my reluctance with Pastor Lyndon, and he confirmed what I had heard in my spirit: "I envisioned you at the microphone, and you were publicly casting down idols. I see this as another step in breaking the enemy's hold."

That pivotal moment came on my own back porch. Cyndi came out excited to tell me about an open-mic poetry night.

"You should go," I said, thinking it would be a great way for her to express herself. "I've written a lot of poetry myself."

Cyndi was all ears as I explained how I'd written most of my poetry during my Wiccan years. Since I had her undivided attention, I went on to share about my own experience.

That's when she told me, "Celeste is teaching me how to do magic."

I was angry, mostly at Celeste, because even in a pagan mindset, training minors, unless they were a coven member's child, wasn't ethical. "You told me you didn't know anything about spells, but I found your charm bag under your bed," I said.

Her eyes grew big. "The charm bag was from Celeste. She gave it to me for protection."

It wasn't until I told her that I was canceling her email account that the turmoil of being out of touch with this woman over took her. "No! You can't do this. That's not fair! You can't keep me from Celeste!" Cyndi screamed.

I firmly stood my ground. "The account is already canceled, and for now it's going to stay that way."

The strange things were, I was seeing myself in Cyndi and for the first time I realized the bondage I hadn't believed existed. My heart ached as I watched this young girl refuse godly advice. I couldn't help thinking of my pastors' efforts in vain to convince me, and how they would probably smile now in light of my revelation.

—⁓—

As the time passed midnight, I grew increasingly concerned. Cyndi had missed her curfew and hadn't called to check in. After waiting another fifteen minutes, I went up in her room to search for the cell number of the friend she was with. Cyndi had left her diary open under her pillow.

I was tempted to pick it up but decided against it, so I slowly pulled the pillow back and read her most recent entry: *Whiskers is curled up so innocently at the bottom of my bed with her bright eyes lovingly looking back at mine, but yet I can't resist this urge to want to put my hands around her neck and strangle the life out of her.* I don't know how long I stood there, reading it over and over and not wanting to believe what I was seeing.

I got up and looked frantic around the room for any sign of our cat. "Whiskers? Here kitty, kitty," I called, but she was nowhere to be found. Had Whiskers suffered the same fate as Cyndi's brother's dog? I tried to regain my breath and composure, then searched downstairs before coming back up to the bedroom. That's when I heard a meow and turned to see Whiskers coming out from under Missy's bed.

I was so relieved yet angry with myself. I didn't want to kick Cyndi out, knowing firsthand the price of rejection. At the same time, this was far beyond any dabbling with witchcraft. This was a warped mind playing with dark magic. What was I forcing my own family to endure? Was Missy even safe sleeping at night? I felt an enormous amount of guilt as I remembered how I had failed to rescue the kids from Michael's oppressiveness. Dare I risk their welfare once again?

I knew what I had to do. I would call Children's Services the next day.

I got a call from Children's Services before I could call them. Cyndi's social worker wanted to set up a time to talk, and I told her the timing couldn't have been better since I was just about to call her. She went on to tell me that Cyndi complained to her school counselor that she was being mistreated.

"Mistreated?" I said. "What do you mean?"

I could hardly believe the twisted tale she told me: "Cyndi says she isn't allowed to take a bath and is forced to get you coffee in the morning."

I was both angry and hurt. Here, I had brought her in as one of my own and did my best to help her, only to have her attempt to undermine me with lies—just as she had accused her brother.

Her accusations were silly, but her scheming could be quite convincing. What would be next? She had stopped at nothing with her next of kin, even taking him to court.

"We need to talk about finding another place for Cyndi to live," I told the social worker. "She isn't happy living here, and I'm concerned for my family's safety after reading her diary." I went on to share what I observed, and we arranged for her removal from my home.

CbAPTER TbIRTY

—ɯ—

Some would see this drawback as a twist of fate, but I saw it as my day of reckoning. In church that Sunday, Pastor Lyndon spoke on the passage in 1 Samuel where the Israelites disobeyed the voice of God and spared the king and best animals when they were supposed to take over the city and spare nothing. It spoke to my own personal walk as I remembered Cyndi's box of idols and daggers still in my basement. That day, I realized I had a few more of my own idols that had not made it to the last bonfire, and as I sat there, God spoke to me about being transparent.

When the service was over I told Pastor Lyndon, "The word you shared really spoke to me today, and I believe God is telling me to get rid of Cyndi's box of daggers and a few more idols of my own."

"I'm sorry. I have somewhere I need to be after church today," he said, "but you can bring them over next week and we can burn them in the fire pit."

Feeling an urgency to clean house, I put my remaining idols in a clear garbage bag in an act of transparency. The time to break all the idols in my life had come. After devising a backup plan, I called Bo and asked him if he wanted to join me.

"Where and when?" he asked. "Better yet, I'll stop by your house now."

Within minutes, Bo picked me up and we loaded my sledge-hammer, my bag, and Cyndi's boxes from the basement into his trunk. We got on the highway and veered off the all-too-familiar road that led to The Village, but before we reached the bridge, we came to an open gate to a restricted dirt road and pulled over.

"What do you think?" Bo asked with a mischievous smile.

I looked around for any landmarks to place where we were, but nothing looked familiar. "Well, the gate's open, but hold on a second. I've never seen this road before."

"It leads to the river. Let's go for it!"

Bo cautiously started down the hill. He checked the rearview mirror to see if anyone was following, but the gravel road was deserted. We drove through the brush to the river's edge, then got out and unloaded the stuff from the truck. At the river's edge, we found a large concrete slab, the remains of a boat launch. It made a perfect stage for our sacrificial altar.

Bo grabbed a dagger from the box and placed it on the concrete. "Give me the hammer."

I handed the sledgehammer to him.

With his feet apart, he lifted the hammer high above his head and slammed it onto the dagger. Sparks flew as the metal hit, but the dagger remained intact. He tried again, this time using his body weight as he flung the hammer onto the dagger, but only a sliver chipped off.

"Let me try." I took a step forward and reached for the sledgehammer.

He gave me a look of disbelief as he handed it over. "Be careful. I don't want you to get hurt."

I held the sledgehammer over my shoulder like a baseball bat and raised it as high as I could before swinging it. The dagger shattered.

His jaw dropped. "How'd you do that?"

I shrugged. "Beats me. Can you get another one?"

Bo pulled a dragon-handled steel knife from the box and placed it on the concrete. I lifted the hammer again and swung it down, dismembering the dragon.

I destroyed another and another until Bo regained his confidence and asked to help me. He looked determined as he raised the hammer like a jock proving his strength at the High Striker carnival game, but when he brought the hammer down, the idol didn't break. His face reddened with embarrassment as his every attempt failed.

I took over again, swinging the hammer and smashing idols. I was on a mission, and one by one they broke into pieces until there weren't any left. No logical explanation existed for what had happened. He was six feet two inches and 220 pounds, and if he couldn't break them, how could I?

I looked down at the scattered remains on the slab. "We can't leave these here."

"Why not?" Satisfied with the demolition, Bo had his hand in his pocket, reaching for his keys.

"Because they're charged with magical energy." I looked out across the river. "I have to finish this. Let's give them a burial at sea."

We threw all the pieces back in the box, then carried them to the edge of the water. The free-flowing river sparkled like diamonds when on the count of three, we flung the broken pieces into their watery grave.

They fell like hail on the water, creating an offbeat rhythm, and I watched them succumb to the relentless current, plunging to the depths of the riverbed. For a moment, I contemplated if they were gone for good and stared at the rippling river as if anticipating their reemergence. Then I felt it, that joyful bliss I'd experienced on the day I encountered God.

I grew faint as the river became a blur. A blanket seemed to be thrown around me, and I was covered by the arms of love. This love that had capsized me when I least expected it and rescued me in my darkest hour, was the same love that held me now. It was all about love—God's love.

Standing on the banks of what had become my personal Red

Sea, I looked across to the land of bondage that I knew all too well. The sun seemed to cast an open portal across the rippling water. How I'd managed to reach this point, I hadn't a clue. Certainly, it was not of my own accord. My "exodus" had taken me the roundabout way, similar to how God had taken the Israelites the long way to the Promised Land. He knew they weren't prepared to face the confrontation they would endure if they took the shorter route, and He knew me too. At this point, any spiritual conflict could have easily sent me back to my former ways, so its avoidance was crucial in my deliverance.

The sun faded behind the clouds, along with the portal. That ancient passage that opened long ago beneath the full moon was now closed, along with the remaining elements of the idolatry in my life. My time for full deliverance was at hand.

Bo's hand rested on my shoulder, and I looked up into his eyes.

"Let's go," he said softly.

I turned and took my first step, his fingers interlocked with mine as I followed him past the concrete slab, up the overgrown path, and back to the car. We got in and Bo made a sharp U-turn, then drove back through the brush and up the gravel road to the highway.

At first, I sat in silence, trying to come up with a logical explanation for my being able to smash the idols when Bo couldn't. He popped in a worship CD, and the silence became an expression of praise filling my mind and guarding my heart on our drive home.

I needed answers, and after all we'd been through, Pastor John was just the person to talk to. If anyone could explain the unexplainable, he could.

John was quiet on the other end of the line, absorbing what I shared. Then he said, "God wants those who have experienced idol worship to see that they can break these representations of power, and He was demonstrating that through physical impossibilities."

What a revelation! The focused will of a believer to destroy what once had a stronghold, now brought victory.

A WITCH'S ENCOUNTER WITH GOD

CHAPTER THIRTY-ONE

—◊◊◊—

O ne year later ...

I stood on the patio of Judah's Java, a local Christian coffee house and my usual Friday-night destination. Cool wind blew through my hair, and the aroma of freshly ground espresso beans initiated a caffeine rush as I waited for the others to join me. Bo's pastor, Jackson, a youthful middle-aged man with a slight resemblance to Elvis and a passion for Jesus and motorcycles, led the worship night that had just ended. I loved the way the Holy Spirit sweetly flowed and drew us into His presence during praise, and I could easily have spent the entire evening there, except our objective this night was different.

The porch door opened and a troop of eighteen prayer warriors gathered out front, awaiting our command to reclaim the city. Wearing his black leather jacket and carrying his lethal guitar in hand, Jackson deployed us in squadrons of three and we were off. I was grouped with Jackson's wife, Maria, whose trademark attire of a black blazer and red sweater conveyed her confident and bold persona, and my long time tenacious friend and confidante, Bo. Our mission field was the city, and the demonic forces that controlled it were our target.

We walked down the street, passing by an array of bistros, antique shops, and, not surprisingly, the local tarot card parlor. An ominous presence loomed over the area. Even Holy Trinity Church seemed oppressed within its cold stone walls. We passed a couple of historic brick-laden homes with celestial door decor and gargoyles at their entry, subtle signs of a possible pagan residence. Speaking our prayer language, we were led by the Holy

Spirit to our strategic region of intercession. For me, it was a witch hunt, but not as one would stereotypically assume.

Pastor Jackson met up with us on Anderson Street and, strumming his six-string, led us to a divine destination. I recognized the house right away—a blue-gray colonial rowhome with a pentacle wind chime dangling from a porch beam and a van parked out front with a *My other car is a broom* bumper sticker.

In my spirit, I knew this had to be the home of Celeste, Cyndi's magical mentor. "Wait, we need to stop here to pray," I said. For carnal-minded Christians, this could have easily become a prayer of vengeance, but the battle was not against the flesh, so we held hands and asked for Celeste's eyes to be opened so God's truth would be revealed. "Saturate her, Lord," I prayed. "Pour out Your love and mercy upon Celeste, and let her know that nothing she has done will separate her from You." My heart's desire was that she would encounter no less than the same love that had capsized me, allowing her the freedom to choose.

As we turned down the dimly lit alley alongside her house, I silently prayed for Cyndi who now lived in a neighboring community with Angie, a mutual high school friend of Missy. I knew her new foster mom, a Mormon woman who I'd heard was meeting the same opposition to discipline, only Cyndi was now discovering consequences far more severe than any I had implemented. Her high school graduation was a few months away, and from what Missy said, she would soon be on her way down South to where her biological mother lived, in hope of reconciling their relationship.

"Jesus," I prayed, "let Cyndi be set free from the spirit of rejection that has held her in bondage since early childhood, and I ask she would be healed from her mother's abandonment that has left an open wound in her heart. Amen."

By the time we returned to Judah's Java, the other prayer warriors were waiting for us. Pastor Jackson closed the evening with a worship song as the warriors disbursed into the night.

The next day, I called Pastor Lyndon, excited and confident

that he would be pleased to hear about my stepping out in faith during the intercessory prayer walk. After all, it seemed that I was under his scrutiny to move in my giftings despite how I felt stifled with all the watchful eyes that monitored my church performance each week at New Zion.

When he answered the phone, I began relaying what I believed all the church elders were waiting for, my moving in the Holy Spirit: "Last night, I went with Pastor Jackson and a group from Judah's Java on a walk through the city to pray against spiritual strongholds and take back the city for God. We even stopped outside the home of the woman who was teaching Cyndi and prayed for her. I can't wait to see what God does."

"By whose authority did you do this, Ally?" he asked.

"By Jesus' authority." What did he mean by asking me whose authority? Whose authority would I or anyone engage in spiritual warfare with, other than Jesus'?

Tap, tap, tap. It sounded like a pen was drumming on a hard surface, probably Pastor Lyndon's desk. I would have preferred he scold me like a child or yell at me, anything other than his silence and the repetitive clatter.

"Pastor Jackson is planning on a spiritual warfare seminar, and I thought it might be good for me to go," I said, breaking the silence.

"Ally, you could teach the seminar!" he blurted. "Why are you going with another church when you could be doing this in your own backyard?"

How was I to answer that? What did it matter where and with whom, so long as I was obedient to what Jesus called me to do? I didn't have to answer, since Pastor Lyndon said he had to go and ended the call.

I stood there for thirty seconds that felt like an hour, the phone still in my hand.

CHAPTER THIRTY-TWO

—⦿—

B o pulled up to the curb and rolled down the window. "Who you gonna call?"

I climbed in, smiling as big as he was. It felt like I'd just gotten into the Ecto-1 and we were on our first Ghostbusters adventure, only this wasn't some lighthearted comedy. "All joking aside, let's keep an attitude of prayer during our ride," I said and bowed my head.

Bo had a copy of the email he had received from Nettie, the owner of Judah's Java, on the dashboard. I guess the word was out that I was the one to call for ridding your home of unwanted entities. Nettie had forwarded an email from her friend Julie, who ran a Christian coffee house in a neighboring city. Julie was concerned about the multicultural display of pagan statues and plaques throughout her mother's home, but the real clincher was an Ouija board that she believed was causing spiritual havoc. Bo's barely legible notes gave us the directions to her mother's home and the time she'd be expecting us.

Thirty minutes later, we arrived at a modest white ranch-style home. This was it, the place we had been called to minister freedom and be used by God to bring release from the darkness that kept this woman captive in her own home.

Bo rang the doorbell, and a small, dark-haired woman who was on oxygen answered.

"Anita, my name is Bo and this is Ally." He glanced at me. "We're friends of Julie."

Anita opened the door wider so we could go inside. We

stepped into the dining room, and Anita motioned us to sit down at the large table. All four walls had shelving displays that housed finely decorated metallic and ceramic animals, Hindu statues, and other artifacts from various continents. Anita explained that they were souvenirs she or friends and family had picked up during their travels. She went on to say that Julie wanted her to get rid of her treasured possessions but she was unwilling, as she considered them simply souvenirs and art.

All eyes were on me, the former witch, to unveil the truth. "Statues, vases, and boxes themselves are human-made creations that are not demonic in nature, but many times they're used as a storehouse for magical energy or may be the source to release a spell to the recipient. Those engraved with gods or goddesses are not just beautiful pieces of artwork but vessels of magic. So one first would need to discern any spiritual influences before purchasing them, but since they're already here, how easy would it be for you to dispose of them?"

Anita's lips stiffened before she gave her list of reasons not to get rid of them. Obviously, a stronghold was at work and she was neither ready nor willing to part with her eclectic collection. With that, she changed the subject to the main reason for our visit, something that kept her paralyzed with fear.

"I got my first Ouija board many years ago," she said. "I would ask questions, and it would answer. Most of the time, the answers were correct or it predicted a future event. Then one day, something really bad happened, but I dare not talk about it. I was frightened and got rid of the board, but then bad things kept happening—negative repercussions for discarding it."

"What kind of bad things?" I asked.

"It wasn't any one thing. It was a series of bad things, and all because I got rid of the board. I couldn't stand it anymore, so I finally bought a new board at a garage sale. It's the same one I have now and keep in the living room closet. I'm afraid to go in there because the door keeps opening by itself and I hear noises, like faint screaming. My husband closes the door, but it won't stay closed. I awaken in the night and stand in the doorway and peek in only to find the closet door is wide open again."

"Where is the board now?" Bo questioned.

"It's in there." She pointed to a doorway in the far corner of the room. "Come, and I'll show you. You can meet my husband, Joe, while you're at it."

We walked through the doorway into the living room, but Anita didn't go beyond the threshold. Bo greeted Joe, who was sitting in the chair near the closet. The man's head nod didn't exactly offer a warm welcome, as he avoided eye contact and didn't get up. In fact, the discernment in my spirit revealed his oppression.

We returned to the dining room table, opened our Bibles, and began reading Scripture. Soon Joe was heading out the door. That's when Anita said they owned a restaurant and he had to go run the business. We spent the next hour talking and praying with Anita, as well as praying against the spiritual influences in the home.

The time came for Anita to join her husband at the restaurant, and she invited us for a late lunch on the house.

"Before we go, are you ready for us to remove the Ouija board from your home?" I asked.

"Yes, but I dare not go in to get it."

Bo took the board out of the closet, and we all left the house. He put the board in the trunk of his car while I climbed into the passenger seat. "I'll follow you," he told Anita.

To my amazement, Anita left her oxygen in the car. While in the restaurant, she waitressed with ease. Even Joe seemed to have a lighter spirit as he prepared food in the kitchen.

"It's like they're completely different people here," I whispered to Bo.

"No kidding. It's like night and day."

Our mission was accomplished, and with the Ouija board in the trunk and on its way to impending doom, we were off. The board was mute and inactive, now an inanimate object. Bo cut it up with a box cutter and put it in a garbage bag, then threw it in the Dumpster so it would never be used again.

CHAPTER THIRTY-THREE

—⚮—

My heart was heavy as I prayed and called Barbara to make sure tonight's prayer meeting was still on. Lynn had just found out she was carrying a baby boy, and excited as I was, we also needed to intercede for my new grandbaby since testing showed he had a birth defect.

Barbara answered the phone, and I shared the prayer need that I would be bringing up that night.

At first she didn't respond, then she said, "Well ... you need to speak with Pastor Lyndon before coming to the meeting."

"What do you mean? Since when do I need Lyndon's permission to come to prayer meeting?" The old familiar feeling of rejection pricked me.

"We'll hold your daughter and the baby in prayer tonight, I promise you that," she assured me.

This was absurd! I felt like I had just gone back in time and my healed wound of rejection had been ripped open. My hands shook as I went to the computer and checked my email. There it was, as plain as day. Pastor Lyndon wrote that since I seemed to relate better to Pastor Jackson, it would be best for him, New Zion, and me if I were to go to Victorious Life Center instead. How could I respond? Right now, I couldn't because I didn't want anger to rear its ugly head at such a critical time.

I called Bo, who drove right over to pick me up. "I'll take you to my church," he said. "I believe they have their prayer meeting tonight too."

Only a few cars were in the parking lot, so he went inside to see if there was a meeting underway. A men's work night had been scheduled in lieu of the prayer meeting, and Bo shared my prayer need and Pastor Jackson told him to bring me inside. As I entered, the sound of hammering and drilling subsided as the men put their paint brushes and power tools aside to gather around me to pray. The peace of God filled me, easing my weary soul.

Once they finished, Pastor Jackson asked, "Are you still attending New Zion?"

"No, I guess not anymore." I couldn't really explain what I didn't understand myself, but it didn't seem to matter.

"Well, you're more than welcome to come here while choosing where to go. I'll take you under my covering since you shouldn't be out from under it."

At that moment, I remembered a promise God had given me—the reassurance that He would always provide a pastor whenever I had the need. It wasn't about relying on men but about trusting God to provide.

—⟨⟨⟨—

For the next year, I attended Victorious Life Center and sat under one of the most gifted teachers of God's grace that I had ever known. It was a step-by-step experience toward freedom in moving in my giftings, and slowly but surely I began the process of being an active part of a small body of believers.

Then, wouldn't you know it, just when I was getting comfortable in my new church home, Pastor Jackson and the eldership decided to close the church. How did a church do that—simply close and send sixty saints searching for a new church home within thirty days? This had to be some kind of test, like still being able to exhibit the fruit of the Spirit even in the midst of such pastoral pandemonium. That Friday night, a remnant of us gathered together to pray, seek God, and ask for direction. We met again the following week, and soon after we felt led to start a home church. Victorious Life Underground was born.

A home church is truly a growing experience. There was no sitting on the sidelines or waiting for the pastor to give a sermon. The attendees truly are the church in every sense of the word. During the week, we were in prayer to see what God would give us to share during our gathering time, be it a word, song, Scripture, or prayer. From the tiny steps of beginning to feel comfortable in developing a relationship with the church body, God now had me moving by leaps and bounds.

Bo and I became co-founders along with a married couple who were senior bikers. From a spiritual perspective, they were polar opposites, with Maggie riding the edge of the prophetic while Chris remained steadfast to his Catholic roots. Regular attenders were Lenora, who was of Jewish heritage and had a big heart and a desire to know Jesus; Jacklyn, who struggled with the demons of addiction and brought her two born-again teenage daughters; and Joe, a novice bass player who was a Lutheran by day and an emerging charismatic by night. We also had a rotating visitor list of those who popped in without prior notice and brought spiritual food to our table.

Occasionally, we would gather to break bread and join in corporate worship with other home churches. On one Saturday night, we were invited to worship with the Crossroads home church. Our group brought instruments, only to find these believers were into the "soaking" form of worship. They were a dozen strong, and their expression of worship could best be described as a restful meditative time, flat on their backs basking in the presence of the Holy Spirit. Differences with worship aside, we brought forth what the Lord had placed on our hearts.

This was when I first met Elaine. She was held in high esteem by the Crossroads church and took the title of prophetess. Lou, another attendee, led us in prayer, and I closed my eyes along with the others until I heard Elaine whispering to Joe, who was sitting right next to me. I opened my eyes to find her massaging Joe's shoulders in a sensual way.

I turned my head and locked eyes with Bo, whose expression made it clear that I wasn't the only one concerned.

Elaine's prayer then morphed into her testimony. She described how her parents willingly allowed her to go with strangers who took her to a remote place and had her put a knife through a little boy's heart as part of a satanic ritual when she was just three years old. The story was extreme and didn't add up. I mean, wouldn't you be concerned if your three-year old came home late at night covered in blood?

From her descriptions, I likened it to more a case of recovered memory therapy, and what seemed to be memories were imaginations that had been coached to fit a real-life event. I felt a burning passion to cast out the seducing spirit that I believe was at work, yet I was a guest in another home church and certainly didn't want to offend their prophetic voice. I struggled in my spirit but restrained myself and said nothing.

A month later, Crossroads came to our gathering. The living room was our sanctuary as we entered into worship. I waved the flaming red tabret that Joan had given me as an expression of praise and my clarion call for boldness, moving in His anointing. Our celebratory dance shook the wooden floor of the old country home.

Then Elaine interrupted mid-song, "Is this home built on a Civil War battlefield?" Not waiting for a response, she continued, "You should do research on your property. You might be amazed at what you discover." Her face displayed a foreboding smirk.

"Can we stop the music?" Andy cut in.

Bo paused the worship video, freezing the words on the screen's waterfall backdrop.

"There's a heavyset man with a beard sitting on the couch," Elaine said. "He's wearing a Civil War uniform and hat, but don't be alarmed. He's a friendly spirit and wants to stay and chill."

This was bordering on the edge of comical and utter disbelief. I felt the burning passion begin to rise in me once again but remained silent. Andy started pacing and suggested that everyone pray about why this Civil War spirit had come and what message he had for us.

I'd had enough. The Bible plainly says, "It is appointed for men to die once, but after this the judgment" (Hebrews 9:27 NKJV). Dead humans did not remain on this earth as ghosts, and Elaine's Civil War spirit was a demon masquerading as a nine-teenth-century soldier. We had no reason to determine the purpose of the demon, as any message would be purely demonic.

I looked around, hoping that one of my own home church members would speak up, but then it hit me: I was the one that the Holy Spirit was speaking to. This was my Kairos moment! I stood and faced the group. "I'm sorry, but this is outright demon-ic." Then I confronted the spirit: "I rebuke you, lying spirit, and cast you out from this place in Jesus name!"

Elaine kept silent. At first her eyebrows constricted, but then the grimace lifted and her expression became peaceful. Andy stood still without uttering a word.

The intense silence broke when Maggie exclaimed, "Amen! Thank you, Jesus!" Several others followed suit, confirming my discernment.

I'd finally done it! I'd stepped out, empowered by the Holy Spirit and as a minister of Christ, and took hold of the keys of the kingdom, knowing "whatever you bind on earth will be bound in heaven, and whatever you loose on earth will be loosed in heav-en" (Matthew 16:19 NKJV).

EPILOGUE

The deck board lifts with each tilt of the rocker, repeating a rhythmic motion that melts away the stress of a hectic work day. Don't get me wrong, it's a small price to pay for the peace of mind that I now possess and a far cry from living in poverty. I squint as the sun beats down. The heat didn't become unbearable until the old maple tree came down last winter, taking the shade along with it. That was the tree that once held the hammock swing that hugged me in its polyester womb during what I call the "dark time" in my life. I've now been out of the Craft for longer than I was in it. In some ways, it seems so long ago and yet like it was just yesterday.

The gate creaks followed by a bang. Titus, my black lab, springs up with a cautionary growl and runs to investigate.

"Hello, anybody home?" Bo calls.

He remains the closest man to my heart, although I remain single. It's funny now to think about it, but for years I dreamt of the day we would wed and I would ride off into the sunset with my knight in shining armor. Today I'm content with us being co-heirs of Christ.

"I'm on the deck. Care to join me?"

A few seconds later, a steady thump dances across the deck and Bo plops in the lawn chair next to me. Cool wetness nudges my hand, and I reach down to stroke Titus's furry muzzle. "Good job. You're a good watchdog."

His tail beats against the wooden rail.

"Did you get that email I forwarded to you from the woman with the Wiccan friend?" he asks.

"Not yet, but I'll check as soon as I get back inside." I survey my backyard, gazing past the last standing tree to the field beyond. Years ago, I stood there, captivated by the full moon that ushered me onto the path of the ancient ways.

"What do you see?" he asks.

"My past."

"Oh. That's where it all began, isn't it?"

"Well, yes and no. It really began six years earlier with the blood-soaked carpet at the bottom of my stairs."

Bo leans forward like a child waiting for his favorite movie to begin. "Tell me, where do you think the blood came from?"

"I don't know. I guess it came from me. All I remember is the image of my motionless body down below and the eerie conversation. How can I ever forget the question that stirred within my soul and the admonition that I would go into the enemy's camp?"

"In your wildest dreams, did you think that you'd end up becoming a witch?"

"No. It's as difficult to fathom today as it was back then, but that bewildering prophecy came true the night I stood out there beneath the full moon."

"Where do you think the prophecy came from?"

"I'm not sure. It was a three-way otherworldly conversation. At the time, I sensed there was an angel and a demon, possibly Satan himself."

Bo's eyes grow big.

"It was kind of like my own Job-like experience—you know, when the angels and Satan presented themselves before the Lord."

"But why you?"

"That's the big question. Someday God may choose to reveal His purpose in that stairwell, but as it stands now, I don't have a clue. All I do know is that I was pre-warned that there would be suffering and pain in my life, and that happened. I lost the godly marriage I had hoped for. In fact, in the end I lost my husband altogether. My children grew up more influenced by Wicca than the knowledge of the Lord, and we were subjected to poverty, depression, mental illness, and ultimate chaos."

I look him in the eye. "I, like Job, blamed God for what I believed was injustice, accusing him of abandonment. But unlike Job who went to God demanding His response, I sought occult knowledge for answers."

Bo gently touches my hand. "Don't be so hard on yourself."

"It's really a terrifying concept to think that God would have allowed me to come so close to jeopardizing my place in eternity."

"Or did He?" he asks. "You know, with such an extraordinary life story, you could write a screenplay." His smile lightens the mood.

I can't help but grin. "Yeah, right."

The screen door swings open. "Grandmom!" A second later, two sets of arms vie for my neck.

"Easy does it." I wrap one arm around each of them. "I've got a surprise for you."

"What is it, Grandmom?" Kenzie drops her arms, jumping up and down.

Ty loosens his grip. "A surprise? Where is it?" His blue eyes widen as he scans the deck.

I retrieve the brown bag from the small wicker table and pull out their surprise.

Kenzie tilts her head and scrunches her lips. "Balloons?"

Ty shrugs his shoulders, then looks at me for an explanation.

"Perhaps Bo will help you fill them with water," I say.

"Water balloons? Yeah! Bo, can you help us?"

Bo gets up and grabs the bag as the kids dart around to the side of the house to the faucet. Watching Ty move as quickly as he does after the doctors gave him no hope of ever being able to walk is a testament to the power of prayer, which only strengthens my faith.

I ponder Bo's crazy concept—a screenplay. I would rather enjoy the present instead of dwell in the past. I've heard it said that you can't start the next chapter of your life if you keep re-reading the last one. I believe it's time to turn the page to a new day—a new season. Being an ex-witch is a thing of my past.

Looking back, my life dilemma was not the result of my ungodly sin, neither was it God's will; rather, I was right in the middle of man's inadequacy and a heavenly war between God and the opposing spiritual forces. Even more mind-boggling is the fact that everything I'd been advised in that strange conversation actually came to pass. I did walk away from Jesus, but despite the frailty of my mind-set and by His grace, I didn't lose my salvation. God proved Himself to be trustworthy, and with that, I am convinced that nothing in all creation can separate us from His love (Romans 8:38–39).

Nothing.

NOTES

1. Lyric (snippet) used in Chapter 14: William Chatterton Dix, "What Child Is This" (1865)

2. Lyric (snippets) used in Chapter 15: Keith Green, "Asleep In The Light" (Sparrow Records 1978), "So You Wanna Go Back To Egypt" (Sparrow Records 1980), "Create In Me A Clean Heart" (Sparrow Records 1984)

3. Chapter 19, Brennan Manning, "Ragamuffin Gospel" (Multnomah Publishers, 1990)

ENDORSEMENTS

"Taken From The Night by S.A. Tower is a book that will take you on a journey you won't soon forget. Gut-wrenchingly honest, this well-written, true story plunges readers into the depth of darkness and sin, only to swoop in with the Light of the World to rescue and redeem. Not only a great book for adults but for mature teens as well. Don't miss this one!"

- **Kathi Macias**, Award-winning Author of
nearly 40 books, including *Deliver Me From Evil*

"This powerful story upholds the values of transparency and freedom that the Father offers us through His amazing love. *Taken From The Night* illustrates how the power of prayer can break through any stronghold and extend restoration and healing to those bound in darkness."

- **Rev. Robert Stearns**, Executive Director of
Eagle's Wings Ministries

"One truth that does not get much attention in today's post-modern culture is that of the reality of evil. To dismiss the kingdom of darkness and the presence of evil in our world is to do so at one's peril. Resonating at the heart of the simplicity of the gospel is the power to be liberated. This book gives witness to this power. *Taken From The Night* is more than just an individual's story of freedom. It is an invitation to those who follow Jesus to embrace those bound in darkness and engage in a lifestyle of worship and prayer that will set captives free."

- **David Ruis**, Renowned Worship Leader, Pastor,
Church Planter and Author

"This book is a must read for every pastor, church leader, prayer intercessor, deliverance ministry and every believer. All of us need to know the devices of the devil. This revealing, real-life story will raise the hair on the back of your neck and teach you how to minister to those trapped by him."

- **Dr. Larry Keefauver**, Bestselling Author, International Teacher and Christian Editor

"*Taken From The Night* is a book where those of us that have been on both sides of this particular fence can attest to honestly and openly say, "Been there, done that!" S.A. Tower's experience has birthed a trumpet call to awareness and sensitivity to both, Wiccans and Christians, a call to forgiveness, love, patience, empathy, and the compassion of The Ancient of Days."

- **Lupe King**, The Way Out Ministries

"Not your usual "we prayed and it was over!" testimony. *Taken From The Night* is a very well written, non-simplistic, non-judgmental record of S. A. Tower's battle with Wicca. Better yet, her experience depicts a battlefield between the forces of darkness and light, with lots of imperfect people contributing to her ultimate freedom. I would give this book to anyone who needs to understand the appeal of Wicca or has been snagged by it."

- **Mark Pettersen**, Founding Pastor, Vineyard Christian Fellowship of the Peninsula

"My dear sister in the Lord and I have gone through a wonderful journey together–to hell and back! This record of that journey is a brutally honest portrayal of what we walked through, including times when I said to her, "I think I care more about you than you do!" Our extensive telephone debates over her involvement with Wicca covered 10 years and many tears. I pray that you will carry away from this book the certainty that our loving God wants you to have a second chance at life because He makes all things (and people!) new again."

- **L. Arendas**, Spirit and Truth Ministries

"Ben E. King, the gospel artist, said that honesty connects with every person on the streets. *Taken From The Night* will make a huge connection with everyone that reads this book. Ally's story connects with people and confirms the power of God's grace. In an age when a lot of people are looking for reality in all the wrong places, *Taken From The Night* is an inspiring story that will redirect everyone's search back to God. Thank you for your willingness to tell us your story. You have hit the ball out of the park with this book."

    - **Don Milam**, Author of *The Ancient Language of Eden*

"*Taken From The Night* is a firsthand account of one woman's deliverance from the occult written by an author with the experience to tell it. If you or a loved one are struggling to find freedom in Christ, I'd highly recommend reading this book."

    - **Pierre M. Eade**, Pastor of Outreach, Author and Speaker

"There are times in your life when the miraculous happens... landmark moments when prayers are answered and you are left speechless. I can testify that *Taken From The Night* is such a time... because I was there and experienced it too. This book is one of the most documented and authentic true stories you will ever read. Her life was filled with twists and turns, at times scaling the mountain of hope and joy, then plummeting to the depths of anger and despair. In retrospect, it was quite the roller coaster ride, but I wouldn't have missed it for the world!"

    -**Robert Marchuk**, Dwell Publishing

You're invited to engage in the encounter at
takenfromthenight.com

- Communicate with the Author

- Read Ally's Blog, The Insightful Scribe

- Find valuable ministry resources

- You can also interact with the author and other readers on the S.A. Tower Facebook Fan Page.

If you liked *A Witch's Encounter With God*, you won't want to miss S.A. Tower's ground-breaking book,

From The Craft To Christ

From The Craft To Christ serves as a catalytic narrative of hope and redemption for those darkened by the occult. In a world full of moral relativism, cultural decadence, spiritual apathy and darkened by the powers of darkness, S.A. Tower shines the light of Christ on the stand of lives emancipated from bondage by the blood of the Lamb.

~ Rev. Samuel Rodriguez, President - NHCLC/Conela

Available at your favorite book and e-book retailers.

ISBN: 978-0-9849523-4-2 (paperback)

CPSIA information can be obtained
at www.ICGtesting.com
Printed in the USA
BVHW050826300620
582506BV00004B/232

9 780984 952304